Christopher
Matthews

HARDBALL

How Politics Is Played
—Told by One
Who Knows the Game

SUMMIT BOOKS
New York · London
Toronto · Sydney · Tokyo

Copyright © 1988 by Christopher J. Matthews
All rights reserved
including the right of reproduction
in whole or in part in any form.
Published by SUMMIT BOOKS
A Division of Simon & Schuster Inc.
Rockefeller Center
1230 Avenue of the Americas
New York, NY 10020
SUMMIT BOOKS and colophon are trademarks of
Simon & Schuster Inc.
Designed by Nina D'Amario/Levavi & Levavi
Manufactured in the United States of America
1 2 3 4 5 6 7 8 9 10
Library of Congress Cataloging in Publication Data
Matthews, Christopher.
Hardball: How Politics Is Played—
Told by One Who Knows the Game.

Includes index.
1. Politics, Practical—United States.
2. Politicians—United States. 3. United States—Politics and
government—1945-   . I. Title.
JK1717.M33   1988   320.973   88-2164
ISBN 0-671-63160-8

To Kathleen

In all my wardrobe, I could not find anything more precious than the knowledge of the conduct and achievements of great men, which I learned by long conversation in modern affairs and a continual investigation of old.

A wise man ought always to set before him for his example the actions of great men who have excelled in the achievement of some great exploit.

—Niccolò Machiavelli,
The Prince

Like the great Machiavelli, I owe much of the wisdom in this book to "long conversation in modern affairs." Here are some of those who deserve to be acknowledged.

Donn Anderson
Martin Agronsky
Lee Atwater
Ross Baker
Michael Barone
David Broder
Patrick Butler
Joseph Canzeri
Margaret Carlson
David Cohen
Charles Cook
Kenneth Duberstein
Peter Emerson
Thomas Foxwell
Doris Kearns Goodwin
Jeff Greenfield
Peter Hart
Robert Healy
Sven Holmes

Albert Hunt
Congressman William Hughes
Edward Jesser
Mark Johnson
Michael Johnson
Larry L. King
Michael Kinsley
Paul Kirk
Jack Lew
Frank Mankiewicz
Congressman Edward Markey
Harry McPherson
Charles Mellody
Congressman Robert Mrazek
Martin Nolan
Robert Novak

Congressman Claude
  Pepper
Scott Pastrick
Michael Pertschuk
Jody Powell
Gerald Rafshoon
Steven Roberts
Jeffrey Sachs
William Safire
Robert Schiffer

Mark Shields
David Shribman
Michele Slung
Robert Squier
Theodore Sorensen
Richard Sorensen
Terrence Straub
Paul Taylor
Sander Vanocur
James Wooten

I want to thank Barbu Alim, Marcel Monfort and James Bethea of the Library of Congress for their tremendous and timely research assistance; Ellen Boyle, Lee Pendergast and Judy Bartee for supporting me in that most political of all terrains, "the office."

I want to express my particular gratitude to those who opened the doors of Washington to me: Congressman Wayne Owens, Senator Frank Moss, Mary Jane Due, Senator Edmund S. Muskie, President Jimmy Carter, Richard Pettigrew, Congressman Tony Coelho, Martin Franks, and the Honorable Thomas P. O'Neill, Jr., Speaker of the U.S. House of Representatives.

Finally, Hendrik Hertzberg, who made me not only a Presidential speechwriter but a journalist as well; Kirk O'Donnell, who taught me the use of political rules; Bob Woodward, who coaxed me over a tape recorder at a critical time; Brian Richardson for his inspired research efforts; Dorothy Wickenden, who gave style and shape to my manuscripts; Timothy Dickenson, who expanded my vision even as he sharpened my prose; to my dynamic agent Raphael Sagalyn, and to James Silberman, the editor who triggered and directed this explosion of words and battle-hardened wisdom.

Contents

Introduction

Be warned. This is not a civics book. It is not about pristine procedures, but about imperfect people. It is not an aerial judgment of how leaders of this or any country ought rightly to behave, but an insider's view of the sometimes outrageous way they actually do. Its subject is not the grand sweep of history, but the round-the-clock scramble for position, power and survival in the city of Washington.

Let me define terms: *hardball* is clean, aggressive Machiavellian politics. It is the discipline of gaining and holding power, useful to any profession or undertaking, but practiced most openly and unashamedly in the world of public affairs.

This book is also meant to entertain. Lived to the hilt, a political career is a grand and exuberant experience. In the following pages you will enjoy some candid glimpses of how well-known figures achieved their ambitions. You will meet some very unlikely success stories, people who learned the game, played hard and won.

Seventeen years ago, I came to the nation's capital thinking that I knew something of politics. I had been an addict of the electoral game, a true political *junkie*, since high-school days. Even then I was rooting for and against can-

11

didates, cheering their victories, grieving with them on election night. When I went away to the Peace Corps in my early twenties, I maintained the romance from afar. With my late-arriving copy of the *New York Times* "Week in Review" and a few scattered magazines, I would strain to make my picks in the year's congressional elections, even though the results reached my little town in Swaziland days after Americans had gone to the polls. So I should have been prepared for my immersion into the political world of 1971. For years I had stood in awed attention at the grand debate, the daunting personalities, the big-picture spectacle of national politics.

But in terms of political hardball, I came to Washington as a neophyte. I entered a world that was as anthropologically exotic as the one I had just left in southern Africa. F. Scott Fitzgerald once said that the "very rich" are different from you and me. So, I came to learn, are the very political.

Behind those vaunted closed doors lies not only the paraphernalia of power but a distinctive language, which I myself have learned to speak. It is a world of tough old alliances, Gothic revenge and crafty deal-making, but also of marvelous state-of-the-art tactics such as *spin* and *positioning*.

Old or new, the machinations of the hardened, dedicated pol would strike most people as offbeat. Indeed, by the layman's standard, there is little in this book that would be categorized strictly as *on the level*.

In the following pages you will read of raw ambition, of brutal rivalry and exquisite seduction. If the tone is tongue-in-cheek, if some portraits and situations appear too comical for such important affairs, you have caught my attitude precisely: with all its nuclear-age centrality, politics is the only game for grown people to play.

"Politics makes strange bedfellows," wrote the nineteenth-century humorist Charles Dudley Warner. That, we will see, is only the beginning of the strangeness. I have learned firsthand that the notions we harbor of political men—and women—are a poor guide to reality. Not even the cynic is prepared to understand the wheeling and dealing of the true pol:

Expect a raging egotist, entranced by his own affairs, and you are seized with the unfamiliar pleasure of having someone probe with quick interest at your own most intimate longings, plotting your course even before you have done so yourself. Expect to be wooed with favors and he captures you instead with a breathtaking *request*. His real knack, as Machiavelli taught him five hundred years ago, lies in getting you to do things for *him*. Eerily and against your will, you discover that the more you do for him, the more loyal you become, the more you want to invest in *his* career.

Expect a figure of dark passions, fired by revenge, and you meet someone with cold-blooded shrewdness, an uncanny bent to bring the most hated enemy into the tent with him. Expect an argument, and you are blinded by the quick concession; yes, you are right on the larger "principle"—it is the smaller, more tangible points that seem to interest him.

Expect a *swell*, born to well-placed connections, and you meet someone heir to another sort of legacy: the inner drive to meet those he needs to meet. Expect a narcissist and you meet a person who not only exposes his faults but has learned, adroitly, to brandish and exploit them.

Such curious, even quirky behavior sets the political animal apart from the pack. And it's what gives certain men and women decisive power over others.

How many times have you heard a colleague complain that he failed to get a promotion because of "office politics"? Or someone say that she turned her back on an opportunity because she "couldn't hack all the favoritism"?

What about the "backstabbing" and the "sharks" who haunt the corridors of business and professional power? But we all know people who have succeeded swiftly and magnificently while others plod along one yard and a cloud of dust at a time. The fact is, there's a great deal of politics in everyday life.

For nearly a generation, I have worked in an environment where politics is the name of the game. As a U.S. Senate aide, Presidential speechwriter and top assistant to the Speaker of the House of Representatives, I have seen men as different as Ronald Reagan and Thomas P. "Tip" O'Neill play the game with gusto and win. I have gained something even more valuable than a healthy Rolodex of connections: the knowledge that success is only rarely based upon the luck of looks, money or charisma. There is energy, of course. All great pols have that. But what drives this energy is the willingness to learn and do whatever is necessary to reach the top. The more they succeed at their trade, the zestier they become. John F. Kennedy and Richard M. Nixon were rivals for office, but they had one great love in common: the contest itself.

Like others before me, I have been fascinated with the towering legends: Lyndon B. Johnson, Franklin D. Roosevelt, Abraham Lincoln. I have heard the tales of how these great politicians learned to forge alliances, make deals, manipulate enemies and bolster their reputations, all the while building strong networks of alliances.

Yes, there are *rules* to the game of power, part of the political lore passed from one generation of leaders to the next. This unwritten code accumulates year by year, like the morning-after cigar smoke in Capitol Hill cloakrooms. You hear it invoked behind the scenes, when someone does it right and pulls off a victory or does it all wrong and pays the price. One of the old-time guys, the fellows who have won for decades, offers the quiet verdict "Just goes to show that . . . " Then comes the sacramental intonation of the rule itself, dredged from the archives of those whose lives depend on winning every time.

I was standing one day in the Democratic cloakroom, that narrow hideaway just off the floor of the House chamber of the U.S. Capitol. The room is equipped with a snack bar, banks of telephone booths and two rows of worn leather couches with pillows so that members can take afternoon naps. It was lunchtime and the smell of steaming hot dogs filled the air. A small crowd of congressmen, escaping the Capitol's chandeliered formality, was lined up munching sandwiches at the stainless-steel lunch counter. The talk, as always, was of politics. Quietly, I confided to one of the members that I was writing a book about the rules of politics, including all the tricks I had overheard in off-the-record hideaways like this. He looked at me, a crease of pain crossing his forehead, and said with dead seriousness, "Why do you want to go and give them away?"

My answer is that such trade secrets are valuable not just to the aspiring pol. There are also enduring human truths in the rules that politicans play by.

In every field of endeavor, there are people who could easily be successful but who spend their entire lives making one political mistake after another. They become so absorbed in themselves that they ignore the very people they would most like to influence. Rather than recruit allies, they limit their horizons to missions they can accomplish alone. Instead of confronting or seducing their adversaries, they avoid them. In making important deals, they become obsessed with intangibles and give away the store. They become crippled by handicaps when they could be exploiting them.

Some might say these tendencies are only human. But such tendencies that pass for human nature, our hesitancy to ask for things, our unease in the face of opposition, are instincts for accommodation rather than leadership, the reflexes of fear. By following them, we trap ourselves. We teach ourselves to stay in line, keep our heads down: the age-old prescription for serfdom.

The premise of this book is straightforward: To get ahead in life, you can learn a great deal from those who get ahead for a living. Climb aboard *Air Force One,* and you will find a world not all that different from your own workplace. People are jockeying for position, all the while keeping an eye on the competition across the aisle. Spend some time in the Oval Office and you will find it much like any other office, much as the Congress is like other large, complex organizations. There are friends and enemies, deals and reputations being made. And there are gladiators, people who keep score by the body count around them. Once you learn the rules, you will have the street smarts not only to survive the world of everyday politics, but to thrive in it.

There is nothing partisan about the right way to get things done politically. As the great mayor of New York, Fiorello La Guardia, used to say, "There is no Republican way to collect garbage." What we are discussing here is not political philosophy but practical method, not why, but how.

When President Richard Nixon faced the imminent prospect of impeachment in late 1973, he took a careful reading of the situation in Congress. The House of Representatives, he realized to his sorrow, was controlled by a Democratic Majority Leader whom Nixon had come to recognize as a fierce adversary. "I knew I was in trouble," the fallen President said from the ruins of his career, "when I saw that Tip O'Neill was calling the shots up there. That man plays hardball. He doesn't know what a softball is."

Hardball is not a collection of political pinups. You will find some of the masters immediately appealing: Abraham

Lincoln, Franklin D. Roosevelt, Dwight D. Eisenhower, Ronald Reagan. It is easy to figure out how the debonair Jack Kennedy succeeded. He had only one handicap, his religion, and managed to turn even that to his advantage. It is harder to discern how Richard Nixon remained at the center stage of American politics for three decades or to explain how Lyndon Baines Johnson, a man with no apparent public charm, could so effectively dominate the United States Senate for eight years. Here it took more than good fortune to offset the awkwardnesses, the odd appearance, the strange temperament; it took a master's passion for strategy and tactic.

Say what you will about how politicians score low in polls of public esteem. There is a Big Casino flavor to their lives that interests even the most disapproving observer. Perhaps it arises from the crackling clarity when the count comes in, when dreams are made and humiliation is dispensed with mathematical exactness. I have known the simple, clear elation of victorious election nights when political careers were born. But I remember, as well, the bleak, claustrophobic feeling on President Jimmy Carter's helicopter as it flew him to Plains, Georgia, that morning of November 2, 1980: it was like being on the inside of a huge, lumbering bird that was dying.

There's a magnetism to this world of make-or-break. I don't know how many times I have stood in the back of a grand hotel ballroom and watched a roomful of adult business executives sit in rapt attention to what some politician had to say. When the time for questions arrives, the crowd dutifully asks about upcoming legislation or the next Presidential campaign. But what's really on their minds is what they smell: power. *What's this guy's story? How did he get where he is?*

Those are good questions. This book is filled with the surprising answers.

PART I

ALLIANCES

Chapter One

It's Not Who You Know; It's Who You Get to Know

> They never take the time to think about what really goes on in those one-to-one sessions. They see it as rape instead of seduction; they miss the elaborate preparation that goes on before the act is finally done.
>
> —LYNDON B. JOHNSON

When I arrived in Washington, Capitol Hill was one of the most dangerous places in town. There was a dirty old map hanging in the Capitol police station marked with little *x*'s for all the corners, sidewalks and alleys where people had been murdered recently.

Life on the Hill had become so precarious that a fleabag hotel near Union Station offered a special cafeteria price to all local policemen: all they could eat for a dollar. With the constant threat of holdups, the management of the Dodge Hotel liked having the view from its cash register blotted with blue uniforms.

By the spring of 1971, the Dodge had already been targeted by the wrecking ball. It was ending its days as a cheap place for buses to stop, an affordable overnight for the senior-class trip. In the tourist guide, its one remaining star was for location.

As I would come to learn, the Dodge deserved at least one more star for history. What happened there one winter

21

more than half a century ago belongs in the first lesson of
any political education.

In the Depression days of 1931, the Dodge had become
a boarding hotel, accommodating several U.S. senators and
at least one Supreme Court justice. It also housed a less
glittering tenantry. Two floors below the lobby level, there
stretched a long corridor of cubicles, all sharing a common
bath. At night this dank underworld came alive, percolat-
ing with the dreams of young bright-eyed men lucky to be
working for the Congress of the United States.

One of the subterranean residents was a gawky twenty-
two-year-old giant with elephantine ears who had just become secretary to Congressman Richard M. Kleberg, Democrat of Texas. Just two weeks earlier he had been teaching
high school in Houston. Now, his first night at the Dodge,
he did something strange, something he would admit to
biographer and intimate Doris Kearns in the months just
before he died. That night, Lyndon Baines Johnson took
four showers. Four times he walked towel-draped to the
communal bathroom down along the hall. Four times he
turned on the water and lathered up. The next morning he
got up early to brush his teeth five times, with five-minute
intervals in between.

The young man from Texas had a mission. There were
seventy-five other congressional secretaries living in the
building. He wanted to meet as many of them as possible
as fast as possible.

The strategy worked. Within three months of arriving in
Washington, the newcomer got himself elected Speaker of
the "Little Congress," the organization of all House staff
assistants.

In this, his Washington debut, Johnson was displaying
his basic political method. He was proving that getting
ahead is just a matter of getting to know people. In fact, it
is the exact same thing.

Before I came to understand the workings of Capitol Hill, I had a hard time comprehending how someone like Lyndon Johnson could rise to such heights. The man was hopeless on TV, sweating and squinting at the Tele-PrompTer with those ridiculous granddaddy glasses. His notorious personal behavior—flashing his appendectomy scar, picking his beagles up by their ears, conducting business enthroned on the john—did nothing to improve the image. Yet there he was in the turbulent 1960s telling us, his "fellow Americans," of the grand plans he had for us. Like many a college student of the era, I was stymied by the riddle: How in a functioning democracy could this figure have climbed over dozens of appealing, able and engaging men to make war and shape peace?

In the years ahead I would come to appreciate how Johnson's mastery of person-to-person dealings, what professionals refer to as *retail* politics, worked so well in the world of Congress and why it works so well in other organizations.

Lyndon Johnson grabbed and wielded power not in the bright glare of TV lights but in the personal glow of one-to-one communication. We will see later how Franklin D. Roosevelt and Ronald Reagan won power through radio and television. The Texan made his most important sales at the *retail* level, one customer at a time.

Those who pray for power have no greater role model than the towering, towel-draped figure standing and kibitzing in the Dodge Hotel bathroom back in '31.

For Lyndon Johnson, Capitol Hill would be a wonderland of retail politics. The critical factor was the small number of people he had to deal with. In this sense it resembled the politics of any institution, whether it be a business corporation or a university faculty. Where FDR made his mark giving "fireside chats" to millions of radio listeners, LBJ worked his magic in the flesh. The smaller the group, the better. Though he spent a decade in the House of Representatives, Johnson did not become a powerhouse until reaching the Senate. It is easier to retail a hundred senators than 435 congressmen.

"From the first day on, it was obvious that it was his place—just the right size," his longtime aide Walter Jenkins remembered.

To clock Johnson's political ground speed in that body it is necessary to mark only two dates. He joined the Senate in 1949. He had won the job of top Democratic leader by the end of 1952.

Johnson's march to power in the Senate began just as it had in the basement shower room back at the Dodge: he went directly to the source. To succeed at staff-level politics, he had checked into the hotel with the biggest block of votes. His grab for Senate leadership began the same way: getting a hard sense of where the power lay. As Theodore White put it, LBJ displayed an instinct for power "as primordial as a salmon's going upstream to spawn."

Brains as well as instinct were at work. While the minds of other newly elected senators in 1949 were awhirl with the cosmic issues they would soon be addressing in debate, Lyndon Johnson concentrated on the politics of the place. After all, the Senate was just like any other organization he had joined. There were the "whales" who ran the place, and there were the "minnows" who got swept along in their wake.

One of the lessons Johnson had learned during his apprenticeship years in the House was the importance of party cloakrooms.

The word "cloakroom" is in fact a misnomer. Members have had offices, where they can presumably leave their coats, since the early part of the last century. The contemporary function of the cloakrooms, which are closed to all but members and a few trusted staffers, is that of daytime hangout. In addition to the snack bars and the well-worn couches, the cloakrooms house a vital set of congressional switchboards and the trusty "manager of phones." Despite his title, this person is far more than a functionary. Better than anyone else, he knows the answer to that relentless question of Capitol life: *What's going on?* He knows when the day's business will end, what's coming up tomorrow and whether the scheduled Friday session is worth staying in town for. If you want the scuttlebutt, or simply to read the mood of Congress, you know where to go. What gas stations are to small Southern towns, cloakrooms are to the Capitol. In every business there are such spots, where people forced to play roles in the workplace stand at ease and discuss the well-recognized realities.

The cloakroom is Congress's water cooler. Lyndon Johnson, the country boy from Texas, knew the importance of such hideaways. The first thing he did after his election to the Senate was to summon to his congressional office the twenty-year-old page who answered the phones in the Senate Democratic cloakroom. His name was Robert G. "Bobby" Baker and Johnson knew this particular young man's talent for sizing up the strengths and weaknesses of those who relied so much on him. Baker would know which senators liked to work hard and which ones wanted to get home or somewhere else. He knew the habits, the schedules, the interests, the social demands and the political priorities. That first meeting, which Johnson convened even before he was sworn in as senator, lasted two hours. "I want to know who's the power over there," he demanded of the page, "how you get things done, the best committees, the works."

Years later, by then an aide to Johnson, "Bobby" Baker would make a name for himself as the premier Washington wheeler-dealer. Though his later conflict-of-interest problems would eventually lead Johnson to disown him, Baker

—a man who knew the good, the bad and the ugly in senators' lives—was a huge and valued asset on LBJ's rise to the top.

What Johnson learned from his new young friend was not far from what he expected: that all senators are not created equal, that within the "world's most exclusive club" there existed an "Inner Club" of Southern senators led indisputably by Richard B. Russell of Georgia. Jealous of its influence, this Inner Club would smash anyone or any group that challenged it. Lyndon Johnson decided then and there to "marry" Richard Russell.

He could not, of course, be too obvious in his courtship; there were other men of ambition who had tried that and learned the pain of unrequited love. Johnson would be more discreet. His first move was to get appointed to Russell's committee, Armed Services. This would give him the excuse he needed to spend a lot of time around the senior Senator without appearing to be currying favor.

That first gambit proved to be enormously successful. He soon managed to make a name for himself on Russell's committee by going after waste and inefficiency in the Pentagon. He had found a way to be both a supporter of a strong national defense and a critic of the military establishment.

Johnson pursued his relationship with the powerful Georgian beyond the professional level. Russell, a bachelor, would have both breakfast and supper at the Capitol dining room. "I made sure that there was always one companion, one Senator, who worked as hard and as long as he, and that was me, Lyndon Johnson," he reminisced at the end. "On Sundays the House and Senate were empty, quiet and still, the streets outside were bare. It's a tough day for a politician, especially if, like Russell, he's all alone. I knew how he felt, for I too counted the hours till Monday would come again, and, knowing that, I made sure to invite Russell over for breakfast, lunch, brunch or just to read the Sunday papers. He was my mentor and I wanted to take care of him."

It was not merely a friendship of utility. Johnson came to develop a tremendous respect for his patron. Years later he would say that the Senator from Georgia should have been President.

But Johnson clearly had his own agenda. While still a freshman senator, he was perfecting a brand of politics still celebrated among political veterans as the "Johnson treatment."

Where the modern, wholesale politician has a tendency to *broadcast* to those he is addressing, as if each human being were a particle of some great undifferentiated mass, Johnson kept close track of the differences among people. He always made a point to know exactly whom he was talking to. Like the future Speaker Thomas P. O'Neill and others of the old breed, he tried to be a kind of political traffic controller, always aware of the direction not only of his own vector but of all the other little dots on the screen. [It may seem all the more surprising that a man with his towering ego should have climbed to such heights by studying the inner as well as the outer needs of others. Yet it was his willingness to focus on other people and their concerns, no matter how small, that contributed to the near total-communication or at least access Johnson achieved with those he sought to influence.]

Jack Brooks, a Texas congressman who had been a close friend of LBJ and knew the "Johnson treatment" firsthand, told me that it came down to an extraordinary ability to concentrate the entire mind on his target's immediate situation. "Lyndon Johnson would convince you that your concern, no matter how small it might seem to other people, was the most important thing in the world to Lyndon Johnson."

Playwright Larry King, author of *The Best Little Whore-house in Texas*, remembers his own experience with Johnson in 1959. At the time, King was working as an aide to Texas Congressman J. T. "Slick" Rutherford, who was very much in LBJ's sphere of influence. One night Johnson came through the Congressman's district as part of a tour to lock up the state for his reelection to the Senate in 1960. He planned to run for President that year and he didn't want to have any distractions at home.

King was less than exultant when assigned to care for the visiting dignitary, and Johnson himself quickly lived up to his reputation as a demanding s.o.b. Standing over a hotel toilet, with the door wide open, the Senate Majority Leader barked out against a background of biological noises a long list of people around the country whom he wanted King to telephone "in the order I'm giving them to you!"

But King had already had his fill of the care and feeding of Lyndon B. Johnson. He left the phone list sitting on a table near the bathroom door. When Johnson reemerged, King, his Congressman and others in the local political party came to attention before a Johnson enraged by the neglected calls.

"Who did I tell to make those calls?" Johnson demanded.

King, equally wrought up, replied, "Look, Senator, the list is on the table. I'm busy enough being lackey to one member of Congress, I'm not going to be lackey to two."

King's boss, stricken with fear, hustled his aide out of the room, mumbling excuses about "the boy" being "tired and overworked." "Go out and get a drink, go anywhere," he said to King once they were safely out in the hall. "Just stay out of sight till he leaves town early tomorrow morning."

At six o'clock the next morning, King crawled into bed.

At six-ten, the phone rang. "Had your coffee yet?" Through the haze, King could recognize the husky and unmistakable voice of LBJ. Arriving at the scene he had been hustled out of the night before, King was greeted by a Johnson standing in a room scattered with the morning newspapers. From the looks of things, he had already been up for an hour.

"How do you take it?" demanded the giant figure, looming over King, the pot of scalding coffee in his hand. King asked for cream and sugar. "I take it black," Johnson said as he poured King a cup of unadulterated java.

Larry King was about to undergo the "treatment."

"Now, I used to be a young man like you," Johnson began, standing so close that King's glasses were fogging, "and I know what it means to be working for someone else and yet wanting to get on and be your own boss. What's your training?"

When King said he had been a newspaperman, Johnson was unimpressed. "Not much money in that. You should go to law school. You can always go back to journalism if you want to, but you'll have the degree."

King never knew for sure why the great man had summoned him for this thirty seconds of predawn fatherly counsel. What he does recall vividly is the picture of himself, the don't-take-shit-from-no-man Larry King, dutifully lugging the Senator's baggage down the stairs and then going back to ask whether there was anything more he could carry.

Johnson had not only transformed an adversary into a bellhop, he had also recruited a future minion to the LBJ campaign team.

Theodore Sorensen, who wrote great speeches for John F. Kennedy and stayed on briefly after Dallas, described the Johnson method of personal dealings this way: never bring up the artillery until you bring up the ammunition.

In other words, to gain a senator's vote on a bill, Johnson would spend days studying every conceivable source of motivation. When he was ready, he would just happen to bump into him. The fellow never knew what hit him.

Few were immune to the treatment. Paul H. Douglas, the great economist who became a great senator, was once opposed to LBJ on a pending vote, but doubted his own sales resistance. "I'm not going out on the floor," he told an aide. *"He's* going to convince me."

On rare occasions, Johnson would launch into his famed treatment without having done his homework.

Russell Baker of the *New York Times* was witness to one such instance. One day in 1961, Baker, then assigned to covering the Senate, was standing in the hall when Johnson grabbed him by the arm and hauled him into his office. *"You,* I've been looking for *you.* I just want you to know that you're the only reporter that knows what's going on around here, that if it weren't for me Kennedy couldn't get the Ten Commandments through this place."

As he commenced his harangue, Johnson scribbled something on a note pad and called in his secretary, who took the note, went out, and returned with it. For an hour and a half, Baker listened in astonishment to Johnson's unexpected tribute to his work and talent as a reporter.

Afterwards, Baker learned from a subsequent visitor to Johnson's office what the message was that the Vice President of the United States had scribbled on that note he slipped to his secretary: "Who is this I'm talking to?"

The secret to Johnson's success, then and later, was his jeweler's eye for the other man's ego. Just as he had patiently introduced himself to one staff aide after another at the Dodge, the future Senate Majority Leader would give the same personal attention to his colleagues in the 1950s. Even as President he would employ the same exhaustive method in gaining approval of the most massive, historic legislative program since the New Deal: Medicare, civil rights, tax reduction and trade expansion. These landmarks were a tribute to this one man's commitment to political retail. When it came to winning, LBJ had the patience and the humility to work each legislator one at a time. "JFK would call five or six," House aide Craig Raupe recalls, "LBJ would take nineteen names and call them all." Such painstaking retail paid dividends: where the dashing *wholesaler* John F. Kennedy had been stalled in his tracks on Capitol Hill, the Great Retailer would get his way.

Lyndon Johnson was an avid student of others' success. He wanted to learn all the tricks. "What's his secret of getting ahead?" he would ask. "How did he do it?" This is not to say that LBJ's attention to the personal was based on altruism. He loathed Robert F. Kennedy, but this did not stop him from studying every habit of John F. Kennedy's brash little brother once Johnson became President, himself. He knew that Bobby liked to stay up late at Hickory Hill discussing weighty issues of art and politics with his highbrow friends. Johnson always made a point of setting his appointments with the younger Kennedy at 8 A.M. sharp: better to have the little fella as groggy and vulnerable as possible.

When several of the country's editoral writers began writing high-toned critiques of Administration policies in the late '60s, LBJ invited a coterie of them to lunch at the White House. Upon their arrival, they were escorted to the West Wing swimming pool. There they beheld, to their shared dismay, the President of the United States splashing away in his altogether. After protesting their lack of swimming suits, the now fully intimidated men of letters permitted an intimacy of communication with the Commander in Chief they had never anticipated when leaving their desks that morning. They could never again scold him with the same impunity. When it came to establishing rapport with someone, LBJ would say and do exactly what he divined was necessary.

But there are limits to political retailing, as Johnson soon discovered. In the late 1950s, while the new-breed John F. Kennedy was laying the public-relations foundation for wholesale victory in the important Presidential primaries, Johnson was counting on the relationships he had developed in the Senate to carry the day. Unaware of the emerging power of the media, he would sit in a room checking off the list of Senate supporters, acting as if they could deliver their states like precinct captains. "I'm okay in Arkansas, I've got McClellan and Fulbright; I'm okay in . . ." The man who assembled a national strategy won the Presidency; the one pursuing the insider's method became his VP.

Often, Johnson would be on the verge of going *wholesale* politically, then allow his instincts to pull him back. White House counsel Harry McPherson tells how Johnson would often encourage him to write a Presidential speech that captured the "big picture" of the Great Society's goals, and then insist that his aide include Johnson's record in adding to the number of chicken inspectors at the Agriculture Department.

As long as he lived, LBJ was unable to grasp the power of television. Veteran journalist Martin Agronsky, then correspondent for CBS, recalls being summoned to the family quarters of the White House to be told by LBJ himself, eating a late supper in the kitchen, that he wanted CBS to give live coverage to an upcoming dinner he was having for the nation's governors. The dinner would include a question-and-answer period which would give Johnson the chance to make a public case for his Vietnam policies. Agronsky called Fred Friendly, chief of his network's news division, and hastily organized the program. On the night before the broadcast, Agronsky was again summoned to a kitchen scene at the White House, but this time Johnson wanted the program canceled because Mrs. Johnson thought that putting the dinner on television would "abuse the hospitality of the White House to the governors." Johnson was willing to pass up this rare prime-time TV opportunity in order to ensure his personal courtesy toward the governors, their wives, and last but not least, Mrs. Lyndon Baines Johnson.

Few politicians today would make such a choice. New-breed pols, their instincts honed to the age, fly toward television cameras like moths to a lightbulb. Still, even in the era of Boss Tube, smart politics begins with learning the basics of one-to-one communication. Johnson knew that the key to success is sometimes not to think big, but to think small, that the best way to feed a giant ego is to feed first those of the people you need to influence.

Howard H. Baker, Jr., who served as Senate Republican leader in the early 1980s, shared Johnson's realism about the Senate, if not his success. "The most important part of a Senate majority leader's education," he once remarked after years of leadership frustration, "is over by the third grade: he has learned to count."

Some of Johnson's successors have understood how to use this basic, retail truth; others have not. When Jimmy Carter ran for President in 1976, he ran against Watergate, bureaucracy, red tape, the arrogance of power, and the establishment. All of this was conveyed in a single code word, "Washington."

Carter's decision to "run against Washington" was a brilliant bit of political positioning. It allowed him, a member of the party that had dominated Washington for most of the previous generation, to posture as the "out" candidate. It gave him the populist edge that carried him to victory against a well-liked Gerald R. Ford.

But his mistake was to allow this anti-Washington posture, so formidable out in the country, to hinder his effectiveness once in the capital. It is one thing to run against institutions. It's another to declare war against the very people you are going to have to work with. No President can carry out a program if the Congress refuses to pass it in the first place, or if the bureaucracy refuses to support its vigorous execution. "People don't do their best work while they're being pissed on," an old Washington hand once remarked to me.

The professionals still wonder, therefore, why Carter's top people allowed themselves the luxury of walking over the congressional leaders they would soon be imploring for support. The Speaker of the House, Tip O'Neill, was told that of course his family and friends could have tickets to the Inaugural Ball, but they'd be in the back of the hall!

That single incident with O'Neill—embellished over time—plagued Carter's relations with the congressional leadership for four sad years. Jody Powell, Carter's closest aide, later acknowledged that the new Administration "neglected the social" back in those early days, and it hurt. It would have been better if they had worked the establishment a bit. "We simply had no group of supporters around town who would reflexively come to our defense," he admitted.

Not all of this was accidental, of course. In crafting his early White House image, Jimmy Carter made much of his effort to deflate the "Imperial Presidency," which had become a major national concern during the years of Vietnam and Watergate. One stunt was his decision to abandon the convoy of limousines and walk down Pennsylvania Avenue in the inaugural parade. A less successful gambit was his selling the Presidential yacht, *Sequoia*. For years, Presidents have found that nothing else loosens up difficult members of Congress like a quiet evening cruise down the

Potomac. As one White House lobbyist put it, getting rid of the *Sequoia* was the "stupidest thing Carter ever did." It gave the new President a short blurb in the newspapers for being careful with the taxpayers' money; it cost him a great deal more at the *retail* level.

Ronald Reagan did it differently. He too ran against "Washington." More than that, he said that "government is not the solution to our problems, it is the problem itself," not a phrase to win the hearts and minds of the city devoted entirely to the business of government. Yet, learning through Carter's mistake, he did not make a vendetta of it. No one ever got the message that the new President was aiming his barbs at him.

The first thing Reagan did after being elected was attend a series of well-planned gatherings in the homes of the capital's most prominent journalists, lawyers and business people. The initial event was a party the President-elect and his wife, Nancy, gave at the F Street Club. The guests were the "usual suspects" of Washington political society; in other words, they were mostly Democrats. "I decided it was time to serve notice that we're residents," Reagan told the *Washington Post*'s Elisabeth Bumiller. "We wanted to get to know some people in Washington." They went to dinner at the home of conservative columnist George Will, where they met Katharine Graham, publisher of the *Post* and *bête noire* of recent Republican Administrations. Next, they attended a party thrown by Mrs. Graham at her home in Georgetown. All this sent a clear signal: the Reagans and their people had come to join Washington society, not scorn it.

The social courtship paid lasting dividends. As late as July 1987, President Reagan served as chief toastmaster at Mrs. Graham's seventieth-birthday party. Carrying his wineglass to the head table, the President tilted his head in characteristic fashion, smiled to the lady of honor and said in his practiced Humphrey Bogart style, "Here's lookin' at you, kid."

Reagan launched a similar *offensive de charme* in the direction of Capitol Hill.

Each year, the members of the House of Representatives, Republicans and Democrats together, hold a quiet little dinner in one of the employees' cafeterias. It is sponsored by the men who manage the House gym, a congressional gathering place, like the cloakroom, where the members are cloistered from the outside world. There younger members play pickup basketball. Older members get rubdowns in the steam room, a place Tip O'Neill never went to without a handful of cigars to pass out.

At the gym dinner, the fare is top-of-the-menu diner food —steak, baked potato, salad, apple pie for dessert. There is no program. The members simply come, serve themselves from a buffet, grab a beer, and find a seat at one of the many long tables. They talk, greet friends—many former members make it back for the evening—eat, talk some more, and leave. In an immensely political world, where congressmen send stacks of "Regrets" every day of the week, attendance at the gym dinner is huge and enthusiastic.

When I attended my first such dinner in 1981, I was surprised to see two other guests: George Bush and Ronald Reagan, the latter in a sporty glen-plaid suit. They had come for no other apparent reason than to share a drink and have their pictures taken with the members. George Bush, a congressman in the '60s, knew the significance of the dinner and what a hit his new boss would make there. He knew that the members would be particularly taken with the fact that Reagan had come to an event that is an inside affair, off limits to the media.

Jimmy Carter never attended a gym dinner.

Reagan, whose contempt for government dwarfed Carter's, was not about to make personal relationships suffer because of political or philosophical differences. He made an effort to win over that permanent Washington "establishment" that can either help an Administration or grease its decline. Despite the fact that he continued to campaign relentlessly against "Washington" as if he had never visited the place, he didn't feel the sting of local rebuke that was visited on his predecessor.

The lesson is obvious. If you want to do business with someone, don't forget the personal aspect. The problem with new-breed pols is that in learning the skills of broadcasting they have forgotten the skills of schmoozing.

I remember my own first conversation with Ronald Reagan. He had come to the House chamber to deliver the 1982 State of the Union address. It is traditional that the Speaker's ceremonial office serves as the Presidential "holding room" on such occasions. Greeting Reagan, with whom Tip O'Neill had been holding a daily political slugfest, I tried nervously to break the ice. "Mr. President, this is the room where we plot against you," I offered, perhaps too gamely.

"Not after six," Reagan beamed. "The Speaker says that here in Washington we're all friends after six o'clock."

The fact is, as novelists and screenwriters love to illustrate, a great deal gets done in Washington simply on the basis of after-hours relationships.

Early in the Reagan Administration, for example, I was asked by journalist Nicholas von Hoffman to help keep a guy from committing suicide. The object of his concern was Mitch Snyder, a political activist who would later become famous as a crusader for the nation's homeless. At the time, Mitch was engaged in a less celebrated cause. He was on the fiftieth day of a hunger strike, protesting the naming of a nuclear attack vessel the *Corpus Christi*. Unlike the Pentagon officials who make such designations,

Mitch did not think "Body of Christ" a fitting title for a U.S. warship.

As it turned out, I was able to help. I knew that despite Tip O'Neill's many fights with President Reagan over national economic policy, he had established a cordial relationship with Reagan aide Michael K. Deaver, whom he had met one night at the home of columnist Mary McGrory. The Speaker had even sung a few songs that night with Deaver accompanying him on the piano.

O'Neill called Deaver to check into the *Corpus Christi* matter. When Deaver returned the call, I told him the story and said the Speaker would appreciate anything he could do. The Presidential aide was noncommittal; in fact, he seemed to be put off by the whole idea of the protest.

Apparently, his interest was greater than it seemed. A few days afterward word leaked back to the Speaker's office that Deaver had gone to see Reagan directly and with dramatic effect. The President overruled his Secretary of Defense, Caspar W. Weinberger, and personally changed the ship's controversial name to *City of Corpus Christi*. Mitch Snyder, settling for this secularization of the ship's name, started eating again. The President avoided a major PR problem, to say nothing of having saved a life.

In Washington there is a term for personal networking: it's called "access."

Senator John W. Warner of Virginia offers a classic look at how the pol can build such access. His classmate at Washington and Lee University recalls him spreading out the folders of the freshman class at Sweetbriar, Mary Baldwin and other nearby girls' schools. Warner then checked the names and faces against a copy of the *Social Register*. Eventually he married the granddaughter of Andrew W. Mellon, founder of Gulf Oil and Alcoa.

Washington is a city built on such less-than-spontaneous liaisons.

When I came to town in the early 1970s, Capitol Hill was little changed from what it had been a half century earlier. It was the same world of retail politics that young LBJ had discovered from his command post in the Dodge Hotel basement. I was also fully aware, of course, of the age-old aphorism "It's not what you know; it's who you know." Like so many others before me, I took it not so much as a warning as a motto and guide to action. If you don't know someone, *get* to know him. That's what campaigns are for.

As I began knocking on Capitol Hill doors, I was hit by the relentless use of a word I had not heard since high-school civics: "patronage."

Every employee, from general counsel of the most prestigious committee to the guy driving the subway cars between the Senate office buildings and the Capitol, owed his job to a particular senator. Sons and daughters of friends back home operated elevators that had been automated for years. There was even a well-dressed young man who sat all day at the basement level of the Dirksen Senate Office Building, and whose job was to wait until a member of the world's greatest deliberative body emerged from the elevator. He would then rise from his chair and ask whether the gentleman or lady intended taking the Capitol subway; if so, he would push a button on the wall behind him, alerting the subway car drivers. Then he would return to his chair.

To get anywhere in this sprawling bureaucratic plantation you needed to have a "patron." To find one, you needed to know which of its patrons, 100 senators and 435 members of the House, to cultivate and what to say to them. No patronage, no job.

I myself came to the Hill with the general ambition of working my way up the political system. My immediate goal was to become a legislative assistant to a congressman or a senator, the job Ted Sorensen had held with John F. Kennedy, and I wanted to end up where he had gone. With two hundred dollars left over from my Peace Corps "readjustment" check, I started to knock on doors.

Since I had no connections, I made a list of Democratic congressmen and senators from the Northeast. My initial targets were those congressmen serving on the Foreign Affairs Committee. I figured they might go for my two years' experience in Third World development. Soon, after distributing fifty or so resumés along the halls of the Capitol office buildings, I began to sense what I was up against. I began looking for some small edge. Having gone to a Jesuit college in Massachusetts, I searched the *Congressional Directory* for members of a similar stripe. Exhausting the Democrats, I began looking to the Republicans. The important thing was to get a job. I was getting down to my last hundred dollars.

Finally, I got wind that Representative James M. Collins, a red-hot conservative Republican from Texas, was looking for a legislative assistant.

Here was one liaison not destined to endure. From the moment I walked into the interview, it was culture shock. Attired in Sun Belt suit, gleaming white shoes and the kind of haircut they give at barbershops with Old Glory in the window, Jim Collins discharged a lightning verdict: "I would say that people of my district, and I don't mean any offense by this, would be put off by your way of speaking." Then, turning to his aide: "Roy, wouldn't you say that people from back home coming in this office would look at this young man and figure he brought back some idealistic notions with him from the Peace Corps?"

Finally he asked, "Who do you know?"

When I mumbled that I knew a guy working in a patronage elevator-operator job, he realized I had my work cut out for me. He then offered some advice that bolstered my growing beliefs about political retail.

"You should try some of the Northeastern, big-city offices. I'll bet there are a good number of congressmen who would like to have someone with your background working for them."

The decision behind us, Congressman Collins added some sage wisdom. "Politics," he said, "is just like selling insurance door to door, which is what I used to do before getting into this business. Some people will go for you and some won't. You knock on a hundred doors, you get nine people to invite you back for a sales pitch. Of the nine, three will buy the policy. You only have to sell three people to do all right, but you'll never find those three unless you knock on the hundred doors to start with."

Two weeks later, lightning struck. With eighty dollars left in the till, I went to work for Senator Frank E. Moss, Democrat of Utah. His top aide, Wayne Owens—now a congressman—had been an assistant to the late Robert F. Kennedy, and, sure enough, Wayne *liked* my background in the Peace Corps. Needing someone with a knowledge of economics, he offered a tryout. I was to take home with me a letter that the wife of the director of the Utah Symphony had written to the Senator asking about the tax situation of people working for nonprofit organizations.

On Monday, after a feverish effort to secure the correct information from Internal Revenue, I was given my reward: I was to be a Capitol Hill policeman, with a daily watch running from 3 to 11 P.M. I was to spend my mornings and early afternoons working in Senator Moss's office. "At least it will put groceries on the table," said my new friend Wayne. He had a point. To win the race, you must first register as a starter.

My education in politics and life had begun in earnest. I

had learned my first lesson in political retail: the importance of one-to-one relationships.

Through seventeen years in Washington, it has been my experience that most opportunities result from a single, identifiable human being.

From 1981 through 1986, I enjoyed an exciting and highly visible stint as senior aide and spokesman for House Speaker Thomas P. "Tip" O'Neill, Jr. I would never have gotten *that* position, which brought me into the thick of top-level Washington, had I not (a) been one of President Jimmy Carter's speechwriters, and (b) worked with a fellow named Martin Franks. Marty had been research director for the Carter reelection campaign. When the Reagan crowd came to town, he became director of the Democratic Congressional Campaign Committee. One of the first things he did was ask his boss, Congressman Tony Coelho of California, to hire me as a "media consultant," which really meant helping Speaker Tip O'Neill, the classic political retailer, fend off the attacks of the world's greatest political wholesaler, Ronald Reagan. Within three months, O'Neill's then top assistant went on to public relations, and the Speaker gave me his job. More than that, he gave me his trust. The next six years allowed me the kind of rough-and-tumble view of Washington politics you could never get with a political science Ph.D.

The chain extends further. I had been named a Presidential speechwriter in 1979 by Hendrik Hertzberg, to whom I had been introduced by a friend of mine from New York, Robert Schiffer, now a successful investment banker and political fund-raiser, whom I had originally met while working in a campaign in Brooklyn six years earlier.

I went to work in the Carter White House originally because a friend, Patricia Gwaltney, had been named to a top position at the Office of Management and Budget to work on Jimmy Carter's pet project, government reorganization. I had met Pat as a fellow staffer on the Senate Budget Committee, to which I had been named by the committee chairman, Edmund S. Muskie of Maine, on the strength of a phone call from my earlier boss Senator Frank Moss of Utah. "You want a good man? Here's a good man."

In Washington, as in most places, building a career is the same as running a campaign. What distinguishes it from an election campaign is the size of the audience. *Retail* is the name of the game. To get ahead, there is usually one identifiable person who matters. Get that person's vote and you've won the prize.

This is how it works in politics and in most other places. If there is another way to get a job than getting someone to give it to you, I have yet to come across it. Just as the legendary Lyndon Johnson demonstrated to us in the john of the old Dodge Hotel, the trick is to find your target and zero in.

It's not who you know; it's who you get to know. The applications of this rule are universal. I did not set off to work my way through the Washington political world by getting a job as a moonlighting Capitol cop under the patronage of a Mormon from Utah, but it worked out that way.

Chapter Two

"All politics is local."

The worst thing you can say about a politician or anyone else with ambition is what House Speaker Sam Rayburn once said of the elusive and professorial Woodrow Wilson: "Wilson was a cold snake. No, snake's not the word—cold fish. He'd look at you cold and steady through those thick glasses. He loved people in the mass, but I don't think he gave a damn about them as individuals."

Tip O'Neill, even his adversaries would admit, never stood accused of such a charge. His long rise to one of the country's most contested positions through a half century of successful elections was built on something hard and elemental. It is the nugget of wisdom prized by all great political figures: to understand and influence your fellow man, don't focus too much on the grand, intangible issues; keep a tight watch on what matters most to him or her personally.

Tip O'Neill has a favorite phrase for this principle: "All politics is local." If you want to understand how a politician behaves, look at what affects him at home, back where his voters are. Politicians use the same hard-nosed approach in dealing with one another: if you want to hurt someone, hit him where it matters to him the most, in his own backyard.

Charles W. Colson, Richard Nixon's most intimate political confidant, was himself a firm believer in the rule. The man known for fierce political dedication—"I would walk over my grandmother if necessary to help Richard Nixon" —also had a keen sense of political motivation. "When you have 'em by the balls," he once observed, "their hearts and minds will follow."

Colson's language and sensibility might stand some refinement, but the logic is unassailable. People look at public issues through the prism of their own welfare. They may care passionately about the starving in Ethiopia, but their vote rides closer to their own stomachs. As Harry Truman used to say, "It's a recession when your neighbor loses his job; it's a depression when you lose yours." The veteran pol worries about the neighbors back home. He keeps his eye on the mundane world of those who elect him. The intellectual thinks *wholesale,* studying public life in all its mighty design; as we saw with Lyndon Johnson, the veteran pol has a penchant for *retail*, one customer at a time.

When Congressman William J. Hughes of New Jersey won his first election, back in 1974, he began holding "town meetings" to keep in touch with the people at home. At the first such meeting, held in his home area of Salem County, the freshly minted legislator opened with a statement of his congressional duties. "I represent you at the federal level," he said. "I don't take care of your potholes. I don't pick up your trash."

When it came time for questions, a woman in the first row raised her hand insistently. "Well, I want to tell you," she began, "they're supposed to pick up my trash on Thursday afternoons and they never do and the dogs get into it."

"You know, madam, as I indicated to you, I'm a *federal legislator*," Hughes told her. "I work on the federal budget and national issues. And what you should do is contact either your mayor or your local commissioner of public works."

Without a hint of sarcasm, the woman looked her hot new Congressman directly in the eye and said, "I didn't want to start that *high*."

If there exists a sacrament of baptism in the secular world of politics, it is administered in such public moments as this. The cold water of truth is splashed in the face of every young pol: you don't tell people what to worry about; they tell you.

Sometimes, the "All politics is local" admonition gets delivered with a vengeance.

Back in 1970, old Congressman Edward J. Patten, from the other end of New Jersey, faced what outsiders thought to be a tough primary challenge by a well-connected anti-war candidate. The septuagenarian incumbent, hopelessly bucking the tides of opinion on the Vietnam War issue, had one thing going for him: his opponent wasn't a "local" fellow.

Just as the primary campaign was getting under way, Eddie Patten ran an ad in the local newspaper. It was nothing fancy, just a reprint from the Manhattan telephone directory with his primary opponent's name and West End Avenue address circled. The challenger was out of the race before he had even unpacked his carpetbag.

Ten years later, the people of Oregon presented the same harsh accounting, this time to a veteran incumbent. Al Ullman, chairman of the powerful House Ways and Means Committee, should have held the seat for life. He had attained great status and power among Washington movers and shakers. Unfortunately, he did not spend enough time back home in the Great Northwest. He was attacked by his Republican opponent for (a) no longer owning a home in the district and (b) having made only six visits to the district the previous year. Ullman shot back that he had been back home "ten" times. In the age of jet travel, when most congressmen get back to the district every other week, Ullman's defense was a flop.

Some of the great names in modern American politics— J. William Fulbright of Arkansas, Frank Church of Idaho, Albert Gore, Sr., of Tennessee are the first that come to mind—met similar rejection when the people sensed that their young hopeful had done more than make good in Washington, D.C.: he had caught himself a bad case of Potomac fever, becoming more familiar in the salons of Georgetown than in the meeting halls back home.

The smarter professional never lets this happen. It's not so much that he makes sure to come home often enough; it's that he gives people the sense that he never left town in the first place.

Lawton Chiles, the three-term Senator from Florida, rejected the well-tailored dark-blue suits so fashionable in D.C. "When I dress like that," he once told a staff member, "no one comes up to me at the airport to say hello." That's why Chiles wears country-cut suits. The man who won election by walking the length of Florida wants to remain in appearance as in reality the same fellow the folks elected.

Without necessarily knowing it, the Florida Senator was observing a basic political tenet first publicized by Niccolò Machiavelli in 1513. Machiavelli warned future politicians, in *The Prince*, to stay close to the people they are ruling. If the politician is "present, in person, he can discover disorders in the bud and prevent them from developing," he wrote almost almost five centuries ago, "but if he is at a distance in some remote part, they come to him only by hearsay and thus, when they are got to a head, are commonly incurable."

Slade Gorton was elected U.S. senator from Washington

State in 1980. For Gorton, it turned out to be a one-term career. Judged by national standards, the young Republican was a first-class legislator. He won good reviews from the D.C. press corps as a thoughtful, independent, hard-working fellow who should have a great future in the Senate. But on the eve of his reelection campaign the Administration named the state of Washington as the place where the United States would dump its nuclear waste. Gorton lost. Unfortunately for him, all politics is local.

The rule works just as smoothly in the positive direction. In 1981 Congressman John B. Breaux of Louisiana admitted publicly that he had been influenced to support the Reagan Administration's historic tax and budget policies with the promise of higher price supports for sugar, a major product of his state. Asked whether his vote could be bought, he replied brightly, "No, but it can be rented." The idiom and the ethic were appreciated back in Louisiana. Congressman Breaux is now Senator Breaux.

Not everyone relishes the firepower of local economic concerns.

In 1982 a young lawyer for a Massachusetts utility company, with the politically appealing name of Frank McNamara, decided to challenge Speaker Tip O'Neill for reelection, financing his campaign with a million dollars raised from oil interests in Oklahoma and Texas who had little love for the old liberal who had long supported price controls. A bad mistake. In an old industrial region that had long suffered hard winters and harder fuel bills, "Dallas" can be a fightin' word.

To seize press attention, the challenger declared his candidacy on the steps of the U.S. Capitol. As the media event got under way, several young men wearing ten-gallon hats passed through the crowd handing out some relevant literature. "You May Not Know Frank McNamara, But They Know Him in Dallas," read the cover. Attached were the news clips of Mr. McNamara's glittery Texas fund-raiser. The next morning's *Boston Globe* contained a short account of the McNamara announcement—but not too short to do full devastating justice to the scene-stealing Stetson hats and the young candidate's oil connection.

The "All politics is local" rule applies just as much in Peoria as it does in Cambridge. A few months later, in the homestretch of the same '82 congressional elections, Tip O'Neill brought a $1 billion jobs bill to the House floor. Republicans mocked the measure as an election-year gimmick. No one was tougher on the Democrats' top man than the House Republican leader, Robert H. Michel of Illinois.

Initially, O'Neill had hoped to avoid any one-to-one combat with his friend Michel. But when Michel tore into the bill as the worst sort of Democratic boondoggle, the Speaker's staff did some quick research. Courtesy of a helpful local office, it dug up some useful information about conditions in the Republican leader's backyard in Peoria.

Taking the House floor, O'Neill began reading the names and street locations of the bridges in Peoria that were below Illinois state safety standards, each of which would be eligible for repair under the proposed jobs bill the Republicans had been attacking as "make-work," another damned New Deal leaf-raking bill.

As the Speaker read his litany of hazard areas into the record, his words were carried via cable TV directly into the Republican leader's district. Minutes before, Michel had been playing the grand and dutiful role of national party spokesman. Now he was in a local damage-control mode. Red-faced, he stood in the back of the House chamber giving frantic instructions to his press secretary. It's one thing to be a team player for the national party; it's another to expose yourself to a hard political shot that will be playing that night in Peoria. By hitting his rival where he lived, O'Neill translated a *wholesale* debate over national economic policy to the local, *retail* level.

O'Neill's most illustrious predecessor was equally adept at this. Short, bald Sam Rayburn was no matinee idol. They don't carve his epigrams onto dams and high schools. But his quiet capacity to deal with congressman after congressman, again and again, turned the mob scene of the House floor into a disciplined army carrying laws and policies that had seemed unachievable. Almost without effort, he could hit members where they lived. "Sam Rayburn could make a call and the Army Corps of Engineers would go to work," Tip O'Neill would reminisce. "Rayburn would take care of the little detail of an appropriation later."

The legendary Texan was thought to wield the same clout with less benign federal agencies. A call from Rayburn might get the IRS auditors working with the same determination as those Army Corps of Engineers bulldozers. Nervous House members could never know for sure whether or not Rayburn ever actually exploited that power, but they lived in fear of it.

Dan Rostenkowski, chairman of the House Ways and Means Committee, is another true believer in the power of political self-interest. The 1986 tax reform bill was greased along a two-track legislative system. First, the members voted on the bill. Next, they got to vote on the "transition rules," the provisions determining when the various tax changes kicked in, with a tremendous impact on particular industries and regions. Practically every member of Congress had an interest in ensuring that his local industry was given the best possible consideration. Those transition rules put hundreds of trump cards into the hands of Dan Rostenkowski. If a particular corporation became liable for a new tax January 1 rather than three months earlier, on October 1, it could save millions. Similarly, if a tax was to be eliminated, far better that it be eliminated earlier. Members who supported Rosty's position on tax reform could obviously expect a warmer hearing on such matters than someone who had not. Rosty knew this; the members knew it. And so did the corporate lobbyists who might have been thinking of opposing the chairman's reform efforts.

Through years of working among politicians, at both ends of Pennsylvania Avenue, I have never met anyone more attuned to the "All politics is local" rule than the man who coined it. Unlike "the Great Communicator," Ronald Reagan, who has projected his strength through television, Tip O'Neill practiced his brand of politics face to face, one person at a time. Of course, this is not the stuff of network evening news reports; it's more important. The final advice that Tip O'Neill gave to Jim Wright of Texas when he handed over the Speaker's gavel had nothing to do with big-picture media relations: "Members are going to come in to see you with some matter that you will think is the craziest thing you ever heard. Just remember, it is very important to that member. Otherwise he would never have come in with it."

Political amateurs make the common mistake of treating all people the same. The great pol does not make this mistake. He keeps his eyes on the exact pressure point that will get the job done.

In 1940, a Promethean test of wills occurred between two American giants, each with his own agenda. On one side was Franklin Delano Roosevelt, a man who had overcome polio to become the most powerful and dynamic President of the twentieth century. In office for two terms, FDR wanted an unprecedented third. One of the critics of his bid was his ambassador to Great Britain, Joseph P. Kennedy, father of a future President and a political dynasty. The climactic episode came just before the November election. Kennedy had staked out a bold public position

against a third term. He was dead set against Roosevelt's
collaboration with Britain and his apparent determination
to bring the United States into the war against Germany.
Kennedy, an Irish-American with no fondness for the British, felt that FDR was not only bringing America into a
terrible world conflict but bringing us in on the losing
side.

"It has long been a theory of mine that it is unproductive
for the democratic and dictator countries to widen the division now existing between them by emphasizing their
differences," Kennedy had said. "After all, we have to live
together in the same world whether we like it or not." He
had made this committed isolationist, "appeasing" statement in London three weeks after Neville Chamberlain,
the British Prime Minister, signed the infamous Munich
Pact with Adolf Hitler.

Roosevelt saw his opportunity. If he could bring a critic
like Kennedy around, he could go a long way toward sooth-
ing a nation justly and increasingly fearful of war.

Even for the great FDR, his manipulation of the Irish-
American tycoon was breathtaking. On October 16, Joe
Kennedy wrote to Roosevelt asking to be relieved of his
post. Within the week, the President had the matter totally
under control. Nine days before the 1940 election he had
the Kennedys to Sunday dinner at the White House. By
Tuesday, Joseph Kennedy was speaking on nationwide
radio to give the Democratic ticket what many consider
the most effective boost of the campaign. "On Sunday, I
returned from war-torn Europe to the peaceful shores of
our beloved country renewed in my conviction that this
country must and will stay out of war."

The Democratic National Committee ran a newspaper
ad declaring that this "one simple, sincere statement by
Ambassador Joe Kennedy smashed into smithereens [Re-
publican candidate] Wendell Willkie's brutal charge that

President Roosevelt is planning to send our boys to London."

One thing was clear enough. Joe Kennedy did not experience a Saint Paul–style conversion on the big question of America's role in Europe. He had little respect for the British, little interest in the anti-Nazi cause and no love for the President determined to bring the United States into the war.

What was it, then?

The ambassador, as Roosevelt knew, held the highest political ambitions for his oldest son, Joseph Junior. The younger Kennedy had served several months earlier as a delegate to the Democratic national convention, pledged not to FDR but to James A. Farley, Roosevelt's most serious challenger. His career was to be the bargaining chip. Sixteen years later, Kennedy Senior would smile triumphantly to his Republican friend Clare Booth Luce and say, "I simply made a deal with Roosevelt. We agreed that if I endorsed him for President in 1940, then he would support my son Joe for governor of Massachusetts in 1942."

FDR's son James described the Roosevelt–Kennedy summit in hardball terms. According to him, his father laid it on the line: the President would be only too glad to help the young Kennedys get ahead in politics, but for the ambassador to desert the national ticket would be to ruin those boys' careers before they had begun. Great salesman that he was, FDR had found the unique selling point. As it turned out, of course, Joe, Sr. was never able to collect on the debt. His oldest son went to war as a pilot and was killed in a courageous bombing raid over Europe.

Three decades later, another Kennedy was taught a similar lesson in pressure-point salesmanship. As Senate majority whip, Edward M. Kennedy of Massachusetts was the second-ranking Democrat in the Senate. In December

1970 he was up for reelection to that post. He had an unexpected challenger, Robert C. Byrd of West Virginia.

As surprising as it seems, the issue was not Chappaquiddick, the incident two years earlier in which a woman had died in a car driven by Kennedy. The contest focused, instead, on intramural issues. It pitted the heir to Camelot against a classic political retailer.

At home in West Virginia, Robert Byrd dutifully plays the fiddle at country fairs. In D.C. he has a reputation that is every bit as solicitous. No chore is too small if a fellow senator needs to have it done. As one former colleague put it, "If you took out a pencil, he'd sharpen it."

And the job of party whip in the Senate resembles that of a shop steward on the factory floor. This person looks out for the members' endlessly developing problems and interests. If they need to have the schedule changed because of an important event back home, it is the whip's job to see whether something can be done. If a senator cares about an appropriation for a highway through his state, the whip lets him know when the matter is being discussed on the floor so that he can be sure to be there.

Kennedy's strengths and notion of the job were very different from Byrd's. As a political celebrity, the Senator from Massachusetts saw the whip's job in thematic terms. It was a soapbox for him to speak out on the major issues of the day, giving Jack and Robert Kennedy's brother yet another forum for his wholesale brand of politics.

Byrd's appeal was more street-level. At the time, he held the Senate's third-ranking position, secretary of the Democratic Conference. Whenever Kennedy went out into the country to give a speech, Byrd assured him there was nothing to worry about back at the office. Kennedy could count on him to handle the details, the scut work too unimportant to command a great man's attention.

Faced with a choice between a party spokesman and a

shop steward, the members of the Senate chose the latter. To the country's astonishment, they thrust Robert Byrd past the heir to the country's preeminent dynasty. Apparently, most Democratic senators like to have their pencils sharpened.

The most vilified figure in modern American politics used a similar tactic in gaining the treasure he prized most.

Few recognize that Senator Joseph R. McCarthy of Wisconsin held the nation so long under his spell mainly through his understanding of the press. McCarthy knew what time reporters had to file, he knew the pressures they worked under and he exploited that knowledge as no one had ever done before.

In the early fifties, when McCarthy was at his peak, most stories about Congress moved on the wires of the Associated Press, the United Press or the International News Service. The Senator from Wisconsin loved the wires, knowing that wire reporters needed to have a fresh "top" on the current story every few hours for their hourly radio broadcasts or late newspaper editions.

Determined to keep his "anti-Communist" campaign alive, he resorted to a simple tactic. According to *Boston Globe* reporter, Robert Healy, who was present on such occasions, the Wisconsin Senator would head to the wire tickers each afternoon. If the day's story was moving his way, he did nothing. If it wasn't, he would approach one of the wire guys and flip him a brand-new lead, a clear beat on the competition.

"Tailgunner Joe"—he got away with a phony war record by sheer effrontery—realized that reporters are people with jobs. He focused on making those jobs as easy as possible. He never let the big picture, or the truth, keep him from the little picture that often makes all the difference.

McCarthy knew of reporters' fetish for two things: time

and documentation. "I have here in my hand the names of
. . ." was raw meat for the journalists of the day. Fortunately, people soon began to notice that in all those words
McCarthy was spinning out for the wires there was not a
single name of a real, live Communist. Without a legiti-
mate mission, even the best executed tactics can only carry
you so far.

The lesson here is not how to become a megalomaniac,
but how to get things done by focusing on the personal
ambitions of the people you seek to influence. Regardless
of your purpose, you need to learn what the person you are
trying to influence cares about.

A contemporary of McCarthy's made a more defensible
application of the "All politics is local" rule. But his strategy was just as cold-blooded.

In 1950, thirty-seven-year-old Congressman Richard
Nixon was running for the United States Senate from California. His race against the actress Helen Gahagan Douglas would be remembered as one of the ugliest in history.
But it also showcased one technique that is not only effective but completely reputable.

Nixon faced a problem. The Republican governor of California, Earl Warren, refused to support his candidacy,
even though they shared the top of the same ticket. It was
a matter of self-interest. Warren, who would later serve as
Chief Justice of the Supreme Court, relished the notion of
offering himself to the people of California as a figure
above partisan combat. He was also a high-toned sort who
considered himself a social superior of the ambitious
Nixon as well as a potential competitor for national office.
An appeal by Nixon to party or philosophical loyalty would
have accomplished the challenger nothing. Neither was
there a public issue that Congressman Nixon could use to
draw Warren into alliance with him.

Nixon faced another hurdle. Mrs. Douglas, his opponent,

was encouraging Warren's neutrality by not endorsing the Democratic candidate for governor, James Roosevelt.

Nixon and his people saw an opening. They would win Governor Warren's tacit endorsement by appealing not to his party loyalty or his ideology but to a concern closer to his heart: Earl Warren.

A young Republican campaign aide named Patrick J. Hillings, who would later serve in Congress, was detailed to ask Mrs. Douglas at every press conference whether or not she supported FDR's son. Finally, the Friday before election, she fell for the bait. She endorsed Jimmy Roosevelt: "I hope and pray he will be the next governor, and he will be if the Democrats vote for the Democratic ticket."

Triumphant in their ploy, the Nixon people broke the news to a reporter covering Governor Warren. When the journalist asked the governor about Douglas' endorsement of Roosevelt, Warren first refused to comment. Twenty-four hours later, he saw that he could not avoid Nixon's cleverly laid trap: "I have no intention of being coy about this situation. The newspaper reports that Mrs. Douglas hopes and prays Mr. Roosevelt will be the next governor do not change my position. In view of her statement, however, I might ask how she expects I will vote when I mark my ballot for United States Senator next Tuesday."

At this, his pursuers declared victory. "Every voter in California who reads this statement will realize that Earl Warren intends to mark his ballot for Dick Nixon on election day," declared Nixon's gleeful campaign manager, Murray Chotiner.

Nixon, who would never win Warren's friendship, had nevertheless won his help. Acting with high-minded restraint, the future Chief Justice weighed the costs and benefits of helping a man he did not love. Nixon's thumb was on the scale, and Warren could not knock it off.

To summarize: it matters little what terrain you are competing on; the key to winning over allies is to focus on
their sensitive points. A college student should focus on
that great audience of one, the professor. With the right
amount of attentiveness the student can discern what the
teacher thinks and cares about most. The notes taken in
class are the best possible guide not just to the course but
to the person giving it.

The same goes in the world beyond school. Regardless
of your religious or philosophical preference, you cannot
afford to be a solipsist, someone who believes he exists
alone in the world. Focusing on your own ego is a guarantee of failure. The smart politician never takes his eyes off
the *other* fellow's ego.

We began this chapter with a searing criticism of Woodrow Wilson. Let's end it with a vignette from our country's
second great wartime President, a man renowned for the
radio "fireside chat" but who could be just as warm in
person.

In 1945, the last year of World War II, when James V.
Forrestal was Secretary of the Navy, his seventeen-year-
old son was ordered to duty on an Arctic convoy, and as a
send-off Forrestal obtained a meeting for him with his
Commander in Chief. Like most Americans, the young
Forrestal had little knowledge of FDR's deteriorated physical condition. Stunned by the sight of the weakened man
who had been the great public figure of his life, he mumbled something about the war.

Suddenly Roosevelt, now fully animated, interrupted:
"Don't talk to me about the war. Tell me what you're going
to do after we've *won* it."

It's no wonder Winston Churchill once said that meeting
Roosevelt was "like opening your first bottle of cham-
pagne."

Chapter Three

It's Better to Receive Than to Give

> If you want to make a friend, let someone do you a favor.
>
> —BENJAMIN FRANKLIN

In 1974 I took a short break from the Washington scene to challenge the Philadelphia Democratic organization. Running for Congress against a well-entrenched incumbent, I was buoyed by several hundred student volunteers excited by the prospect of electing to the House an independent candidate not that far from their own age. Still in my twenties, I evoked more enthusiasm than electoral strength, coming in a distant second in the primary.

There was, however, a small consolation. A few days after the primary, I received a letter expressing the urgent hope that I would "stay actively involved in Democratic politics." The clincher was not the condolence but the request that came with it: "I would appreciate any information or advice you might have that would help our efforts in Pennsylvania or other states. Please feel free to contact me personally or Hamilton Jordan. Jimmy Carter."

This was two years before the Presidential election. Carter, governor of Georgia, was serving as chairman of the Democratic Campaign Committee. Coming at the time it did, the letter left a lasting impression.

People are still baffled about how Jimmy Carter got himself elected President of the United States, how this man from nowhere could put together the kind of grass-roots organization needed to win primaries and party caucuses in Florida, Iowa, New Hampshire, Pennsylvania and all across the rest of the country, to the New York convention.

The truth is, James Earl Carter was in those days something of a country slicker. He saw that the voters wanted something different after Vietnam and Watergate. That was the big picture, but he did not stop there. He went countrywide, putting himself personally into a myriad of small pictures, the world in which real voters live. His urban rivals exhausted themselves, meanwhile, vying for the affections of the Democratic party's jaded constituencies in New York and Washington.

We saw in earlier chapters that building personal power or, perhaps more accurately, enlarging personal capacity begins with an initial two-step process: first, pay close attention to what motivates others; second, employ this information to map paths to the "hearts and minds" of those who are critical to our objectives.

The next step is learning how to get those people mobilized in our cause. In political terms, we are about to learn how to build a campaign.

To build a campaign, any campaign, you first need an organization: and Jimmy Carter's creation of a national organization from scratch between 1974 and 1976 was a work of brilliance.

As a lame-duck, single-term governor from the Deep South, Carter was a political outsider who could not rely on the usual Democratic Party network, where national interests, Washington connections and ideological talent combine. He had to create an organization of his own.

His strategy was simple: to build an outsider's campaign, recruit some outsiders to run it for you. I've saved that letter from Jimmy Carter back in '74 till today and I'm not the only one. Every Democrat who lost a primary election that year received a personal letter from the obscure Governor Jimmy Carter of Georgia.

Smart politics. Carter recognized that his best hunting ground for support was among those who had been shut out politically. Jerry Rafshoon, his media adviser, remembers campaigning with Carter for an attractive congressional candidate and telling him that he thought the man would do well. But Carter saw deeper. "He's not going to win. It's a Republican district. He'd be better for us if he loses. He'll work for me. He'll bring his organization with him."

Jody Powell, who was with Carter from the beginning, recalls his boss's forthright explanation: "People who have lost are going to be looking for something else to do. If you get elected, you're going to be a congressman going off to Washington." Powell saw the tactic pay off all the way to Pennsylvania Avenue. "It was not just the candidate but the people working with the candidates. We set up a roving band of people who had some political experience, primarily with congressional campaigns."

Carter pursued his strategy through the '74 general elections. When Robert L. Strauss, then the national party chairman, was calling the Democratic winners on election night, the governor was calling the losers. Many, temporarily shaken and adrift—Richard Pettigrew of Florida, John Gilligan of Ohio, Midge Costanza of New York—joined the Peanut Brigade and, with many lesser figures, played key roles in Carter's dash through the primaries. Those otherwise forgotten candidates who had lost races for Congress became Carter's local coordinators and political cheerleaders.

Glimpsing Carter's strategy of building a nationwide network of political outsiders, Robert Keefe, a veteran political consultant then working for Senator Henry M. "Scoop" Jackson of Washington State, saw its brilliant potential for breaking through the party establishment: "What we have here is a Trojan peanut." Like its ancient predecessor, the horse, it was built because its makers could not storm the citadel. They had to seduce their way through the door.

The high-riding front-runners in the '74 midterm campaigns had no need for some lame-duck governor from the rural South to come liven up their campaigns. They had grander allies, big names like Edward M. Kennedy and Hubert H. Humphrey, to help them build crowds and sell fund-raising tickets—all, of course, in exchange for support in 1976. "It was the underdogs," Jody Powell told me, "who needed Carter"—just as he would need them.

After a generation of bigger and bigger budgets, vaster and vaster television audiences, larger and larger campaign planes, Carter had turned a new key: getting thousands and thousands of voters to feel they had a stake in his victory. As he went from state to state, staying in the homes of campaign supporters, he created strong loyalties. He came to town not as a visitor, but as a guest. As former Kennedy aide Ted Sorensen put it, "How can you vote against someone who slept on your couch?"

Contrary to what many people assume, the most effective way to gain a person's loyalty is not to do him or her a favor, but to let that person do one for you. Again, it was Niccolò Machiavelli who in sixteenth-century Italy discovered something basic about human nature. He observed that when a city was besieged for many months, when the people had lived through tremendous hardship within the city's walls, when they had suffered horror and hunger in defense of their prince, they were all the more loyal to him. They felt even more bound to him afterward, "looking upon him as under an obligation to them for having sacrificed their houses and estates in his defense. And the nature of man is such as to take as much pleasure in having obliged another as in being obliged himself." Or, in another rendering of Machiavelli's wise admonition, "Men are by nature as much bound by the benefits they confer as by those they receive."

Thomas S. Foley, the House Majority Leader, tells the story of the man who rescued him when his small plane crashed in a rural patch of eastern Washington State and, though he had never heard of Foley before, became a relentless contributor to his campaigns. The same bond arises in less dire circumstances. Those who give you one helping hand very often make a habit of looking out for you further down the road. We tend naturally to remember the people we "discover" along the way and seek to ensure that they prove us correct.

When you ask someone for help, you are implicitly asking people to place a bet on you. The more people you get to bet on you, the shorter your odds—and the larger your network of rooting supporters is going to be. But many people hold back because they see each request for help as an admission of weakness and each assertion of self-reliance as a sign of strength. This do-it-yourself mentality can be lethal. It can limit and isolate a contender, denying him allies.

The little secret shared by smart politicians (and appreciated in at least one other profession) is that people get a kick out of being propositioned. The smart politician knows that in soliciting someone he is not so much demanding a gift or service, he is offering the person the one thing he himself wants: the opportunity to get involved. The candidate asking for a campaign contribution or a vote is simply offering a chance to join in the political action, to be part of his success. He is selling stock in himself, and in the process he is creating a network of stockholders.

What the successful politician has is the ability to approach a perfect stranger to ask not just for his vote but for his time, effort and money. He has no hesitation in accosting a wealthy woman at a cocktail party and asking her for five thousand dollars, or in asking others to drop everything and devote themselves to his advancement, saying, "I'd like you to work for me for the next six months as a campaign volunteer," knowing that it would mean the recruits would be working around the clock, for little or no pay, and with no guarantee of a job even if their candidate wins. Politicians develop the attitude admirably and most crudely extolled by that great California assemblyman Jesse "Big Daddy" Unruh: "If you can't drink their booze, take their money, screw their women, and vote against them in the morning, you don't belong in this place."

John F. Kennedy, despite his opulent background and his polished Ivy League reserve, became expert at this exercise. He never went the Elks Club route—wearing funny hats, spending evenings being slapped on the back —but he learned to campaign in a more personal way, trudging up and down the triple-deckers of Cambridge and Charlestown, knocking on doors and asking working-class Irish, Italians and Armenians for their "support."

As a candidate for Congress in 1946, running against a popular local mayor, Kennedy was forced to build a totally independent political organization. It set the mold for all the later Kennedy campaigns. He brought twenty-thousand members of the Boston working class onto the family team. Practically every campaign volunteer became a "Kennedy block captain," armed with a personal supply of buttons, signs, and literature on Jack's exploits aboard *PT 109*.

The Kennedys knew how to dispense their family glamor. Every Irish Catholic mother in Cambridge pressed her daughter to volunteer in order to have a shot at the handsome, wealthy young bachelor. The nervous girls were quickly put to work on some important project, such

as writing personal thank-you notes for "the family." Their
letters might well be addressed to other storefront volunteers like themselves. The addressee didn't matter; what
mattered was the trust implied in the assignment. It was
in such moments of personal fulfillment that the famed
Kennedy organization was created.

In the years that followed, there would be analogous
bouquets for the $500-an-hour lawyer who could abandon
family and career at a moment's call to advance Jack or
Bob or Ted. The tangible reward might be nothing more
than a *PT 109* tie clasp, the outward and visible sign of the
inward and spiritual "Kennedy connection." A man who
had contributed financially for years felt himself fully com-
pensated by having Jack give his mother a kiss. "They
always made sure you were included," Ted Sorensen recalls fondly more than two decades later.

This willingness of one man to go out and boldly *ask*
was the secret fuel of the Kennedy juggernaut in the late
1950s. It explains how a forty-three-year-old senator with
no role in the national party or the Senate leadership could
snatch the Presidential nomination from the party establishment.

What the Senator from Massachusetts did in the campaign was unprecedented: he applied his local technique
of political retail to the Presidential race. He sent his campaign director, Lawrence O'Brien, out into the country
simply to ask county chairmen, small-town mayors and
state AFL-CIO treasurers to support him for President of
the United States. No one had ever asked them before.

"As I look back on my travels, the thing that amazes me,"
Larry O'Brien recalls, "is that we had the field almost
entirely to ourselves. No one representing Johnson or
Humphrey or Symington [the other candidates for the
Democratic nomination] had preceded me to the state
houses and union halls. As I moved from state to state

making friends, I kept waiting for the opposition to show up, but it never did."

On July 13, 1960, Kennedy won the nomination. At ten-thirty the next morning, he offered the other spot on the ticket to Lyndon Johnson. The Texan had played it very rough as adversary for the nomination, attacking him not only for his poor attendance record but also for his bad health, suggesting that Kennedy suffered from a secret terminal disease. Kennedy knew, however, that he needed the Texan as his running mate in order to win big down South. Political experts agree that if he hadn't made that extraordinary decision, Richard Nixon would have been President eight years sooner. Just as the Kennedy forces had proven during the long battle for the nomination, the willingness to *ask* can be the greatest of all power plays. As Lyndon Johnson put it later, even he was overwhelmed by Kennedy's request. "It took a pretty big man to walk down two flights of stairs to ask that of a man who had opposed him all the way down to the Panama Canal."

People don't mind being used; what they mind is being taken for granted. Tip O'Neill often tells a story from his first and only unsuccessful run for office. The year was 1934, when, still a senior at Boston College, he ran for a seat on the Cambridge City Council. On the day of the election, he met a neighbor who said she was going to vote for him even though he hadn't asked her to. O'Neill was surprised at her statement. "I've lived across the street from you for eighteen years," he told her. "I shovel your walk in the winter. I cut your grass in the summer. I didn't think I had to ask you for your vote." He never forgot her response. "Tom, I want you to know something: people like to be asked."

The fact is, the more favors asked, the more supporters recruited. People who pour their souls and their bank balances into another's destiny cannot afford to be too critical.

They simply have too much invested. As Machiavelli suggested, great careers are like great wars: the sacrifices call for further sacrifices.

Paul Corbin, a tough old political operative who spent years at Bobby Kennedy's side, tells a tale about his fundraising efforts for a successful Wisconsin gubernatorial candidate in the mid-1950s.

Early in the Democratic primary campaign, Corbin had persuaded a very wealthy fellow, a registered Republican, that his contribution to Corbin's candidate was essential to prevent a "red" takeover of the Wisconsin Democratic Party. A hefty check soon arrived from this Republican, which supplied the margin of victory in a tightly fought race.

Corbin went back to the contributor during the general-election campaign. Clearly Wisconsin Communists were determined people, he argued. If Corbin's candidate were to lose in November, the party would fall into the hands of "the reds" the next time around. He scored again: big contribution; big victory.

On inaugural day, the contributor showed up at the executive chambers.

The apprehensive governor went right to the point. "I want you to know how much we appreciated your help."

Silence. A *long* silence.

The visitor took in the ornate chamber. Finally: "This is quite an office, isn't it?"

The governor was worried. What does that guy *want?* A road contract? Zoning variance? Patronage? Another interminable pause, then:

"I just wanted you to know," the visitor burst out, "that all those years I was giving to Republicans and I've never once been on the inside of this room."

"If there is anything we can do . . ." said the flabbergasted governor.

"No."

"Isn't there *anything* we can help you with?"

Yet another pause.

"Well, there is *one* thing."

The two pols, the governor and Corbin, braced themselves.

"Do you think I could have one of those low-numbered license plates?"

This is not an unusual story. Even the richest contributor is in a sense a political groupie. The low-numbered license plate symbolizes, after all, a connection with power; the simpler, the better. Membership in the "Eagles Club" was conferred on loyal Republicans in 1980 for giving Ronald Reagan $10,000. If you pay the required amount, in other words, you are not just a contributor, you're a dues-paying member of a real in-group.

A politician will help get someone's daughter into a good college, and the constituent will soon forget (remembering only the other child that the Congressman failed to help with). The same person will never forget, however, that he gave money to the Congressman's campaign. There's an interesting asymmetry in the way contributors and politicians refer to each other. The benefactors call the recipients "friends"; the recipients call the givers "contributors."

Many people spend their whole lives resisting having others do favors for them. In doing so, they forfeit not only the gift directly offered, but something far more important: the power that comes from receiving. Never forget the basic accounting principle at work here: an account receivable is an asset. Those who have helped you in the past are more likely to help you again. Professional fund-raisers value above all the "contributors' lists" of earlier campaigns; their scientifically tested hypothesis is that, when asked, people tend to "back up their bets." Your goal should be to make yourself other people's asset, to build your own "contributors' list."

We live in a debtor society in which citizens, like their governments, build their lives on a whole network of obligation—taking out a mortgage, going to the bank for help to buy a car, etc. Yet the same logic that applies to buying a home or a car or financing a college education is ignored when nonfinancial lines of credit are involved.

The greatest untapped reserves of energy are not under the Arabian Desert or off the north slope of Alaska; they lie in a hundred million underappreciated hearts. The worst sin of a campaign manager is to let a potential volunteer leave headquarters without being given something to *do*.

Make your cause the other fellow's hope; hope is his asset, your opportunity. The more each invests, the more likely each will be to reinvest again and again.

Some people are fearful of accepting help because it may come with strings attached. But it is actually rare that a contribution to a political candidate involves some carefully calibrated barter of money or time for something of comparable material value. The gift more commonly constitutes a deal of a subtler sort: an investment in a piece of the *action*.

Every time I have worked in a political campaign, from Congress to the Presidency, I have felt the same sense of being drawn into the thing, being almost hypnotized by the race itself.

People love to be asked—for advice, for help, for attention in any form; it makes them feel more valuable, more real. It cements a bond. Just as it is hard to vote against a guy who just slept on your couch, how can you knock the guy you've been advising? The prominent Washington attorney Robert L. Strauss, who went from being Democratic Party Chairman in the mid-1970s to U.S. Special Trade

Ambassador in the Carter Administration, is a master of such recruitment.

I remember him walking down the corridor of Philadelphia's old Bellevue-Stratford during a 1980 campaign stop. Suddenly he spots someone he barely knows talking to a perfect stranger. A lesser man would speak to the vague acquaintance, but it is to the new face that Strauss turns with the familiarity of one sidekick to another: "Is he filling you with enough bullshit? I wouldn't believe a word that fellow told me. Not a word."

With a slight crease of a smile to the fellow he recognizes, Strauss moves on. In that one casual moment, he accomplishes a week's worth of fund-raising and party-building.

Here's how it works:

First, the towel snap by Strauss stuns the stranger with the realization that he is talking to the friend of a major national political figure. Until that moment, he had no idea his associate was so well placed. Going by the locker-room exchange he's just witnessed, his friend doesn't just know Strauss, they must have been on Guadalcanal together!

The secondary impact is just as spectacular. Strauss cements a relationship with the fellow he didn't even speak to, may have met only once before, and whose name he may not even remember.

Tom Donilon, a young lawyer who has played a major role in recent Presidential campaigns, was once awakened at his home by Strauss at 4:30 A.M. "Get your ass out of bed, you little left-wing s.o.b. I've got to do the *Today* show in a couple of hours."

To Donilon, this abrupt reveille was "the most endearing thing Strauss has ever done." Being asked advice from a big shot like Strauss beats kind words any day. "Men," Donilon himself surmises, "want above all else to be treated like *men*." All that locker-room language is

Strauss's patented way of letting tough, wealthy men—and the occasional whiz kid—know that they are not only part of the team; finally, they are one of the boys.

Warren G. Magnuson of Washington State was one of the crustiest men to ever sit in the Senate. His campaign slogan, "He Stands Up to the Big Boys," was the very measure of the man. Yet it was Magnuson, the cigar-chomping tough guy, who would tell how, after a long night of card-playing with the boys, President Franklin Roosevelt would pay off his losses with a check, which he would ceremoniously sign, confident that no winner would ever cash it. And, wanting the connection, Magnuson never did.

The old-boy networks, of course, have never been hospitable to women and minorities. The walls of prejudice can be just as strong in a democracy's government institutions as they are in business. Racism and sexism make access more difficult, but the same rule applies: it's always smarter to ask than to wait for someone to give.

During the spirit-numbing Carter reelection campaign of 1980, there was a regular 8 A.M. staff meeting at the headquarters in a half-demolished building on K Street, Washington. Crowded around a cheap folding table on equally cheap folding chairs would sit Hamilton Jordan, the campaign manager, several operatives from labor and the Democratic National Committee, a representative from the Vice President's office, and one of the President's speechwriters.

The daily presence of one visitor, a first-term member of Congress, stood out. Such people, particularly from fading urban districts, are busy: cutting their niche, learning the ropes of Washington, keeping the wolf from the door at home. To come each morning to share the weight of this extra, thankless duty seemed extraordinary.

When I went to work for the Speaker's office in 1981, I

began to notice that this same member of Congress, though elected just two years earlier, was equally ubiquitous in national party affairs: each newly vacant position, whether secretary to the House Democratic Caucus or the Speaker's proxy at meetings of the party's National Committee, seemed to be quietly sought and competently filled by this same member—Geraldine A. Ferraro.

Whatever the ultimate problems with her 1984 Vice-Presidential candidacy, the fact is that she won that historically unprecedented opportunity through her relentless willingness to demand a place for herself. Her secret for gaining repeated access to the political inner circle was elementary: she asked; she received; she became a player. Geri Ferraro became extremely well known within the party as someone who was always on hand when party issues and party leadership were to be discussed. When members complained that she was too damned pushy, Speaker Tip O'Neill would agree—with a characteristic twist: "Sure she's pushy. That's what it takes in this business."

In 1984, Democratic Congressman William H. Gray III of Pennsylvania executed a brilliant political coup, becoming the first black to win a major leadership position in the House of Representatives. For years, black members had held significant positions in "their" areas—civil rights, African affairs, education and welfare matters. None had ever run for mainstream assignments in the areas of national economic policy and foreign policy. Bill Gray broke that mold by campaigning successfully for the chairmanship of the powerful Budget Committee. He sought out those Southern members with the most conservative reputations, making convincingly clear his determination to win and his desire for their active and public support.

In a world where prejudice remains all too real, where many doors to opportunity remained locked from the inside, Geraldine Ferraro and Bill Gray dared to knock, proving that not every door was bolted. They made the other guy say no. They proved that when it comes to gaining power the best hardball is the willingness to *ask*.

I will never forget sitting in the Speaker's back-room Capitol office one night when Senator Robert J. Dole, who lost the use of his right arm in World War II, stood with his cup at the coffee urn and asked whether I would turn the handle for him. As an adversary, Dole can be starkly manipulative. But when I recall him unself-consciously asking me to turn the handle, I feel a stir of fondness for the guy.

I remember, too, being on the other end of a similar relationship. As a young Peace Corps volunteer in rural Swaziland, I would travel from one small trading store to another, offering bookkeeping and business advice. In many cases, the store owner would offer me a warm Coke to drink, it being sweltering and refrigeration being non-existent. That simple act established a bond between us. As those who study primitive cultures discovered long ago, accepting a favor is as important as giving one. No relationship is a one-way street. Along the dusty roads of southern Africa I was unknowingly obeying a rule as tough as Machiavelli's and as benign as Benjamin Franklin's. "If you want to make a friend, let someone do you a favor."

Chapter Four

"Dance with the one that brung ya."

I'm a dyed-in-the-wool party man. I don't know just what party I am in right now, but I am for the party.
—HUEY "KINGFISH" LONG

Loyalty is one of the virtues that conveys political as well as moral worth.

In 1981, a special congressional election was held in North Philadelphia to replace one of several officeholders convicted in the "Abscam" scandal. The winner was Joseph F. Smith, a genuine political regular, the sort who works his way up the local city organization, waits his turn and eventually achieves a position of public honor.

Moments before the swearing-in ceremony in the House chamber, I stood by the Speaker's chair prompting Tip O'Neill with a brief biography on the member-to-be. There was only one point that I figured would be important. I told the Speaker that the new gentleman from Pennsylvania had long been a trusted aide to O'Neill's old colleague Congressman William "Digger" Byrne, the man who had represented the same Philadelphia district a decade earlier.

The feudal tradition ran deep. Byrne himself had succeeded his father in serving the area, first as head of the family funeral business—its friendly motto, Byrne used to joke in the cloakroom, was "We Let You Down Easy"—

and later in the congressional seat. The Speaker asked me whether "the Digger" was still alive. I told him that he had died a few years earlier.

Only someone schooled in the mysteries of street-corner political loyalty could decipher the exchange as the Speaker came face to face with the new Congressman from North Philadelphia.

The Speaker: "So . . . how's the Digger?"

Representative Smith: "Oh, he died two years ago."

The Speaker: "Yes, I heard."

To the casual listener, this might sound like the dialogue from an Abbott and Costello routine. But to an ear more finely attuned to the basic protocol of the street-corner politician, Tip O'Neill was not inquiring about a dead man's health. He was saluting another man's coat of arms. "How's the Digger?" was his way of saying, "I know where you came from. I know your loyalties."

From the outside, politics seems a cutthroat world. Those who run for office stop at nothing. They will question an opponent's motives, his patriotism, even his character. What seldom gets noticed is the deep, feudalistic code that binds the combatants together. To fight the good fight, you need to know that your back is covered.

"Loyalty is everything in this business." From a Tip O'Neill—from any of the old breed—this is not Pollyanna. If you travel to Washington, D.C., you will be struck by one great difference from the other great cities of twentieth-century America: not the presence of monuments, but the absence of smokestacks. Unlike other capitals whose politics visibly depends on a sprawl of factories and assembly lines, Washington produces just two things: the paper currency that we all use and the political currency that politicans use. *Deals* are what people make in Washington, deals pure and simple. A senator tells his colleague that he can count on him for support in getting funding for some crucial public-works project in the other senator's state. He is expected to deliver. If he doesn't, his word becomes worthless. The value of making a deal with him becomes worthless; so does his seat in the Senate. If he doesn't deliver, he can't deliver for his people at home. His "effectiveness" begins to get questioned around his state.

If there is one, mighty lesson to draw from politicians, it is this: nobody trusts a traitor. A man can be a great fighter for his country, he can play a decisive role in a brilliantly decisive battle, as one great American did in the War for Independence, but if he betrays his friends he becomes a Benedict Arnold.

Even in the age of corporate head-hunting, it is one thing to change jobs, and another to show lack of loyalty to someone you once served. Nothing is more self-defeating than trying to win the faith of a new employer by betraying the trust of a former one. Nothing is more impressive than for the fierce competitor to draw the line on such betrayals. As Senator Eugene McCarthy once said approvingly of speechwriter Richard Goodwin, who had served him and then had gone to work for his adversary Robert Kennedy when the latter entered the Presidential race, "Dick's the kind of man who changes uniforms without giving away the signals."

One of Ronald Reagan's great strengths and the foundation of his durability as a politician has been his long-standing ties to the conservative movement within the Republican Party. Beginning in 1964, when he gave his memorable speech on behalf of the desperate Goldwater campaign, Reagan has hammered relentlessly at the same themes. Avoiding the counsel of those who saw more votes in the middle of the road, the Gipper has continued to run down the rightward side of the field.

This earnest stumping for conservative causes paid Reagan enormous political benefits. It saved him when less ideologically observant candidates fell by the wayside. A case in point was his Lazarus-like resurrection in the 1976 North Carolina primary. Given up for dead by the pundits, Reagan reached back into his ideological arsenal and won the hearts of the GOP hard-liners. Here in the patriotic South, where mothers and fathers raise young boys to be officers and gentlemen, the loyal conservative reached for the heartstrings. Fighting Communists was tough business, he declared, and Gerald Ford just wasn't tough enough.

Reagan came back from the dead again in 1980, after his defeat by George Bush in the Iowa caucuses, winning in New Hampshire because the old-line conservatives, the party faithful who had been listening to his radio commentaries for years, stuck to him just as he had stuck to them.

Once President, Reagan continued the courtship instead of taking the marriage for granted. He made a special effort to promote such conservative journals as the *National Review,* by attending its anniversary, and the *Washington Times,* by regularly calling on its correspondent Jeremiah O'Leary at press conferences. He prided himself on sticking with his old crowd through victory as well as defeat. Unabashedly, he appeared at rallies of the most passionate conservative fringe. Speaking to a convention of ideologues in 1985, Reagan said, "I always see this as an opportunity to dance with the one that brung ya."

The only time that Reagan's two-way loyalty to the Republican right ever faltered was in his handling of the 1986 Iranian arms affair. The scandal hurt Reagan more than it might have another leader for the simple reason that this was one time he *didn't* dance with the conservative partner that had brung him. He was caught dancing with the Ayatollah Khomeini.

Loyalty is not simply a virtue, but a building block of

political strength. We saw in the earlier chapters how we can come to command strong alliances by (1) learning the interests and ambitions of others, (2) mapping our way toward helpful relationships, and (3) cementing those relationships with reciprocal support and benefit. Loyalty is the linchpin of this network of support.

More is at stake here than political retail. Betrayal not only destroys relationships, it destroys a reputation.

Some might assert that in the age of media politics, when public records are sold on television, interpersonal ties and loyalties play a decreasing role. What matters, they will argue, is the individual appeal, the ability to communicate an appealing image on the television tube. Recent history suggests just the opposite.

Arguably two of the most charismatic figures in recent American history were John B. Connally of Texas and John V. Lindsay of New York. Both men had first-rate minds and proven skills as media performers. "Big Jawn" was a tall Texan like LBJ, a man's man like Johnson, but everything else was a media adviser's dream: as handsome as his colleague was not, as polished as Johnson was crude. John Lindsay, mayor of New York, lit up the tube like no one since Jack Kennedy; at the same time he was such a show-biz natural that he served as substitute for Johnny Carson on the *Tonight Show*.

Then governor Connally gained national prominence in 1963, when he was hit by the same spray of bullets fired by Lee Harvey Oswald at John F. Kennedy. Nine years later, he won temporary fame once again, leading "Democrats for Nixon." But when tall, handsome, Presidential-looking Connally switched parties to run for the 1980 GOP nomination, nothing happened. He ended up spending $12 million only to elect Ada Mills of Arkansas as his sole delegate to the Republican national convention. More than his connection with Watergate-era scandal, it was Connally's image as a political turncoat that did him in.

The Connally phenomenon happened in reverse when Lindsay, a Republican, tried to become a Democrat. Lindsay, at least, had an excuse for switching. As a candidate for reelection in 1969, he was denied renomination by his own party. To win a second term, he had to run under the banners of the Liberal Party and his self-created "Urban Party."

When Lindsay announced his candidacy for the Democratic Presidential nomination in 1972, there was a great deal of media interest. What no one counted on was the problem of political "identity." As the chairman of the New York State Democratic Party put it, "We're just trying to establish his credibility as a Democrat." It didn't work. In the pivotal Florida primary, where Lindsay's New York connection should have come in handy, Lindsay was mocked for having switched sides. As an opponent, Senator Henry Jackson, put it, "Here's a fellow that's just joined the church demanding to be a member of the Board of Deacons." Lindsay came in fifth in Florida. The next time out, in Wisconsin, the media star came in sixth.

Both men, Connally and Lindsay, it should be pointed out, defected for ideological reasons. But that didn't matter to the voters. Ironically, the more the differences between the two parties seem to narrow, the more important party loyalty becomes to the voter. People may not know the philosophical nuances that separate Republicans from Democrats and may often switch their own vote from column to column, but they know an opportunist when they see one. As a "Democrat for Nixon," Connally had shown star quality. As a sleek liberal under the Republican banner, Lindsay had political sex appeal. He was the pretty girl in the tight bikini. By ending his political tease, he revealed himself as just another liberal Democrat.

Connally and Lindsay are the exceptions that prove the rule: loyalty is the *norm* in political life. A private citizen can change parties every day of the week and no one will even notice; this is not the case with a person whose career has advanced on the shoulders of others. The only honorable, acceptable way for an officeholder to switch parties is to first resign the office to which he has been elected. In 1983, Congressman Phil Gramm of Texas did just this. He resigned his seat, which he held as a Democrat, then contested it in a special election running as a Republican. His success was so dramatic that he was elected to the Senate the following year. By giving back what was given, by evening the books with his constituents and his party, he found a way to avoid the Benedict Arnold taint. He had crossed the lines under heavy fire; his place in the other army was won, not bought.

There are two important corollaries to the "Dance with the one that brung ya" rule.

FIRST: YOU HIRE YOUR BOSS.

When you take a position, in politics or in any other line of work, be very careful. Once you establish a relationship of loyalty, it is hard to back out of it. If you join the wrong side, you will be stuck with the Hobbesian choice of cutting and running or dying in a ditch with a man or a cause that you would never want to be seen alive with.

When I first went knocking on doors on Capitol Hill I came within a whisker of such disaster.

As mentioned earlier, I was advised by a certain Texas congressman to focus my job search on members from a region and background similar to my own. Following my ethnogeographic hunch list, I walked into the outer office of an Irish Catholic Democratic congressman from New Jersey. As a member of the House Foreign Affairs Committee, he seemed like someone who might have a place for a graduate of Holy Cross with recent, first hand experience as a Peace Corps volunteer in Africa.

So you can understand, given my desperation, why my adrenaline began to run hot when this charming Knights of Columbus type walked over to the reception desk and asked whether he could help me.

When I told him that I was just back from Swaziland and was hoping for a job on the Foreign Affairs Committee staff, he cut me short. "No. You should be working as a legislative assistant in my office."

I couldn't believe my luck. As this down-to-earth guy showed me the plaque honoring his sponsorship of the original Peace Corps legislation, everything seemed to be clicking. Only later would I learn that the man had caught the country's attention in a *Life* magazine account of purported mob connections and of the time he allegedly used these connections to have a body removed from his basement.

As it turned out, after several trips to the office of the gentleman from New Jersey, I received word from his ice-cube top aide that "the Congressman wanted me to tell you that he couldn't work it out."

Looking back on the case—within the year, the same Congressman would be convicted of income tax evasion, the first of many legal entanglements—I like to think that this Irish charmer I had met in that long-ago reception area was trying to save my resumé from an association with a political career doomed to ever deeper trouble.

One of the most important rules of loyalty is to commit it to the right person. Once you're aboard, it's hard to ignore the captain. Once you've served, it's impossible to deny *whom* you've served.

SECOND: WHAT'VE YOU DONE FOR ME LATELY?

A relationship of mutual trust can be shattered by something well short of outright betrayal. People lose faith in their allies long before they hoist the enemy flag. Ask any politician and he'll tell you how fickle constituents can be.

This is why smart politicians make repeated efforts to demonstrate their loyalty to the people who support them.

Did you ever notice that swings in the economy neatly correspond to the political calendar? Recessions usually occur in the first year after a President wins an election. Recoveries are timed to reach full vigor as the country is poised for a new political season. A President knows that he must complete his term on an economic upswing. If he is going to squeeze out the inflation and cut some benefit programs, he'd better do it right up front so that the pain is forgotten by the next election.

"Injuries should be inflicted all at once, for the less they are tasted, the less they offend," wrote Machiavelli, "while benefits should be granted little by little, so that they might be better enjoyed."

The second part of this injunction explains why politicians not only try to get the dirty work behind them early but also ensure a regular flow of benefits in the months before election. Those entrusted with office must be seen providing loyal service at the time people are making their judgments on the quality of that service. In 1984, voters reelected President Ronald Reagan by a landslide. They judged him on the strength of the brisk recovery that began in 1983, not the recession from which they were still in the process of recovering. The converse is also true. If a politician is doing badly around election time, it doesn't matter how good he was two years ago.

Case in point: Jimmy Carter. Despite the dangers of inflation, upon taking office in 1977 he moved to stimulate the economy through tax relief and various measures to reduce unemployment. It was not until the end of his Presidency, in the very year he sought reelection, that he tightened the screws. Not only did he appoint the tough-minded inflation fighter Paul A. Volcker to chair the Federal Reserve Board; he took the extraordinary step of withdrawing his annual budget plan and submitting one with dramatic election-year budget cuts. The only more flagrant case of political suicide was the one committed by former Vice President Walter F. Mondale when he announced at the 1984 Democratic national convention that if elected he would raise taxes.

The classic account of the voter's short memory was recorded by Senator Alben W. Barkley of Kentucky, who would later serve as Harry Truman's Vice President. In 1938 Barkley had been challenged for re-election to the Senate by Governor A. B. "Happy" Chandler, who later made his name as commissioner of baseball. During that campaign Barkley liked to tell the story of a certain rural constituent on whom he had called in the weeks before the election, only to discover that he was thinking of voting for Governor Chandler. Barkley reminded the man of the many things he had done for him as prosecuting attorney, as county judge, as congressman and as senator.

"I recalled how I had helped get an access road built to to his farm, how I had visited him in a military hospital in France when he was wounded in World War I, how I had assisted him in securing his veteran's benefits, how I had arranged his loan from the Farm Credit Administration, how I had got him a disaster loan when the flood destroyed his home."

"How can you think of voting for Happy?" Barkley cried. "Surely you remember all these things I have done for you!"

"Yeah," the fellow said, "I remember. But what in hell have you done for me lately?"

The sentiment is universal. People judge the quality of a relationship in terms of recent evidence. Just as a Christmas card can maintain a personal or business tie, the lack of one can undo it.

Politicians can teach us the importance of regular political fence-mending. When they campaign for office, they establish a symbiotic relationship with people and set the tone for an enduring bond: just as they are campaigning neighborhood to neighborhood, they will serve in office on the same basis, returning to the people, checking in with them, listening to what they have to say. Most important, they will keep the relationship up-to-date through a regular show of concern.

Effective politicians know this. Soon after I went to work in the Senate, my boss, Frank Moss of Utah, decided to offer an amendment I had drafted. It dealt with the minimum wage. I had noticed that, over the years, the minimum-wage increases periodically approved by Congress consistently followed rises in cost of living and in productivity. The amendment I recommended to the Senator would have pegged annual minimum-wage increases to these two indices automatically.

I expected it to attract considerable support from pro-labor senators on the Democratic side of the aisle, but it claimed just fifteen votes.

Later I would learn the reason. Democratic politicians were not about to give up the opportunity to raise the minimum wage every few years, the kind of sugarplum that helped them with the working people of their districts and kept labor involved in the party legislative agenda. Putting such increases on an automatic escalator would deny both labor leader and politician these prized opportunities.

For precisely this reason many members of Congress profoundly regret that several years back they indexed Social Security benefits—pegging them automatically to rises in the cost of living—thereby depriving themselves of the opportunity of proclaiming in their quarterly newsletters that Congress had once again increased benefits for the hard-strapped senior citizen. They may also soon wish that they had not indexed the tax system: before, they won much credit for cutting taxes, when all they were really doing was lessening the pace of "bracket creep."

This was a lesson not lost on Representative James A. Burke of Massachusetts. Soon after his first election to Congress in the 1960s, he was asked by his Massachusetts colleague House Speaker John W. McCormack whether there was anything the Speaker could do to help in his district. Yes, said Burke, there was one thing: he wanted to have the federal government restore the home of John Quincy Adams, who after leaving the Presidency had represented the district in the last seventeen years of his life. This would make Jimmy Burke a hero among his constituents.

McCormack asked how much it would cost. "Oh, about seventy-five thousand dollars," Burke replied. McCormack smiled. Given the importance of the project, Burke could count on getting the full amount appropriated that session.

At this point, Burke became concerned. "Could you make it just thirty thousand for now? I don't want to finish the whole job in one year!"

In the early 1970s, Congressman Henry S. Reuss of Wisconsin introduced a bill to create a federal ombudsman to help people cut through government red tape, freeing House and Senate offices of the sometimes frustrating task of helping constituents back home deal with the federal bureaucracy. It sounded like a great idea. Dozens of congressmen enlisted as co-sponsors of the bill. But it went nowhere, because there was no way in hell that the senior members of Congress were going to let some nonelected bureaucrat grab credit for helping people with their governmental problems. That is what congressmen and senators get reelected year after year for doing.

Back in 1932, James A. Hagerty, then a sage political reporter for the *New York Times* and later President Eisenhower's press secretary, offered a similar bit of advice to Jesse I. Straus, the president of Macy's. Straus told Hagerty that he intended to make a major contribution to Franklin D. Roosevelt because he not only supported FDR's candidacy, but also because he wanted a Presidential appointment once the Democrats took office. He was prepared to give FDR $15,000 *up front*—a huge amount measured in today's dollars.

Hagerty was appalled. "That's a substantial contribution," he said. "Don't give it all at once. Give five thousand at the start and indicate they can come back for more if they need it. Halfway through the campaign, they'll be back. This time give them another five thousand and indicate that that is all you intend to contribute. About a week before election, they'll be so desperate for money that someone will suggest that maybe you can be induced to come to the rescue. They'll hesitate to put the bite on you, but they will, reluctantly. That's the time to give them the last five thousand. They will be very grateful, much more than if you gave it all at once and they spent it early."

Straus served for many years as FDR's ambassador to France.

Lobbyists, of course, are professionally adept at stringing out such exchanges. You will never hear a high-paid "Washington representative" tell his corporate client that the consumer movement has peaked, that the legislation the industry had long feared has been permanently tabled. "I think what we've been able to do is contain that particular problem," he will tell his clients in ominous tones, "at least for the time being. But with the right kind of campaign and resources we can keep the matter stabilized." As H. L. Mencken once warned, "Never argue with a man whose job depends on not being convinced." Don't ask a plastic surgeon to compliment you on your youthful appearance.

A good lobbyist learns that his job depends upon his keeping himself necessary. He's not being retained for old times' sake!

Martin Agronsky, who has been covering Washington since the 1940s, tells a New York story that illustrates the city's "What've ya done for me lately?" syndrome rule as well as any.

There was a bagel lady who worked for years on Madison Avenue. For years, a man would pass her little corner stand each morning and drop a quarter into her tin. Not once did he ask for a bagel. After fifteen years of this, the old lady finally stopped him one day and said, "Do you mind if I ask you a question?" Startled, the man replied, "I suppose you are going to ask me why all these years I've been giving you a quarter and never even asked you for a bagel."

"No," she said. "My question is, do you happen to know that the price of a bagel is now fifty cents?"

PART II

ENEMIES

Chapter Five

Keep Your Enemies in Front of You

> Better to have 'em inside the tent pissin' out than
> outside pissin' in.
> —LYNDON B. JOHNSON

The Battle of Saratoga was the decisive victory of the American Revolution. When it was over, and General Burgoyne had given his sword to General Gates, the two armies' officers sat down together at a dinner opulent even by contemporary standards: ham, goose, beef, lamb, "great platters overflowing with many vegetables," and plenty of rum and hard cider.

Had I read of this quaint scene when I was younger, it would have struck me as absurd. Here, after all, were a group of presumably passionate warriors, who just hours before had been aiming their muskets at each other's heart, sitting around a table having a pleasant supper together.

That was before I spent almost two decades working among politicians.

When you look at that meal at Saratoga from a politician's viewpoint, the scene in the American "winner's tent" makes perfect sense. What better way to dampen the fighting passion of the Redcoats than by sending the message that losing isn't so bad after all? Those Yanks aren't such bad blokes once you sit down and share a cider with 'em.

First-rate politicians often take on Horatio Gates's atti-

91

tude. Just as he had "Gentleman Johnny" Burgoyne over to his tent for that delightful get-acquainted evening, so the great congressional pros have awed me over the years by their sheer capacity to deal with opponents of diametrically opposed views. On countless occasions, I have seen a member cross the chamber of the House of Representatives and, having just exchanged red-hot words with an adversary, pat the same guy on the back, trade some irreverent joke, ask about the family and head off out through the lobby.

Once again, there is more at work here than good fellowship. "No eternal friendships," the great British statesman George Canning once said, "certainly no eternal enmities; only eternal interests." Like great countries, great politicians remain on speaking terms even with their fiercest opponents, and for very sound reasons. First, it shows strength. Nothing can be more unsettling to an opponent than some casual chitchat from a guy whose head you have just tried to tear off. Second, it offers useful information. The more you meet and listen to the other side, the more you learn what they're thinking, what they're feeling about you and your side as well as about theirs. Most important, you might just have to work with that guy someday. The opponent in one fight is often the valued ally in the next. The astute politician always keeps the lines of communication humming. As Kirk O'Donnell, Tip O'Neill's trusted counsel for many years, put it, "Always be able to talk."

The smashing success of Ronald Reagan's first term is a testament to this rule of power—and no one knows this better than those of us who were on the other side of the Capitol Hill firing line.

Before coming to the White House in 1981, Reagan had spent most of his career in large organizations. As a contract actor with Warner Brothers and other big studios, as an executive of the Screen Actors' Guild and as a corporate spokesman for General Electric, he had been taught that each member of a big organization has his own part to play. Unlike Jimmy Carter, who except for his tour with the Submarine Service had spent most of his adult years running a small farm and warehouse, Reagan had never been a lone entrepreneur.

This difference in professional background typified their Presidencies. Where Carter spent a good part of his day in self-imposed solitude, doing huge amounts of paperwork and listening to classical music, Reagan worked with a team. As a corporate man, he knew right up front that he did not have to, indeed could not, run the whole thing himself. He never had. When he did *Knute Rockne* or *The Santa Fe Trail*, there was a producer to pull things together, writers to knock out the scripts, directors to keep the action moving, publicity boys to do the hype. The star, of course, was at the center.

And, say what his critics will of him, the old trouper knew his strengths. When he came to the White House, the Great Communicator brought a solid crew with him, a crew recruited for the very purpose of making the most of the star's own talents: good writers, plenty of PR help, even a good director, Michael Deaver, a master of camera angles and backgrounds out on "location." It was Deaver who set the tone for the general-election campaign by picking that wonderfully evocative spot for Reagan's Labor Day campaign appearance in 1980—the candidate in shirtsleeves with the Statue of Liberty at his back. Long before Lee Iacocca had brought back its luster and its place of honor in our American myth, Deaver had seen the Lady's patriotic *launching* potential. In a medium where pictures are worth a thousand words, Ronald Reagan had the best location scouter in the business.

Ronald and Nancy Reagan also knew the new President's weaknesses. He had a huge administrative task before him: a giant bureaucracy to be tamed. That would take a kind of talent that Reagan had never claimed. He would need a strong chief operating officer who could run a tight ship and have the right kind of political strength. To keep the star looking good, he would need more than his conservative philosophy; he would need a good measure of *moxie* as well.

They already had their idea man, Michael Deaver, and their ideologue, Edwin Meese III. What they now needed was a genuine producer, the kind of guy who could pull everything together, and throw a little *class* into the mix.

They found their man in James A. Baker III.

It was a brilliant recruitment. In the months ahead, it would be Baker who would field-manage the new President's 1981 legislative triple play: the largest tax cut in history, the largest defense hike, and the largest cutback in domestic spending. Even old-time Reagan hands would admit grudgingly that the President could not have pulled off this feat without the gentleman from Texas.

What made the initial decision to hire Baker and then to move him into the top spot so spectacular was the man's political background. For years, Jim Baker had been Ronald Reagan's greatest nemesis.

The two initially faced each other from opposite ends of the playing field in 1976, the year of Reagan's first serious run for the Presidency. The incumbent was Gerald R. Ford, who had succeeded to the office on the resignation of Richard Nixon and now after a series of bloody contests was leading in the delegate count for the Republican nomination. With only a few primaries remaining, Reagan attempted an unprecedented coup: he named Senator Richard S. Schweiker of Pennsylvania as his prospective running mate.

Traditionally a candidate picks someone to run with him only *after* he wins the nomination. In breaking the tradition, Reagan said that he wanted to offer the convention a "balanced ticket." His more immediate, tactical motive was to blockbust Schweiker's otherwise pro-Ford home-state delegation, Pennsylvania, and stampede the convention. It was a bold, desperate move, worthy of a man who wanted to be President.

The Ford high command responded to this thrust as Eisenhower reacted to the German drive at the Bulge, throwing in everything they had. Jim Baker was dispatched to break the attack, cost what it might.

Baker was determined to deny the Reagan-Schweiker axis to as many of Pennsylvania's delegates as he could. He launched a furious *retail* campaign to lure one delegate at a time back to Ford. Obscure state senators found themselves having dinner at the White House. Their families became mini-celebrities touring the Cabinet offices. Dams, bridges, hospitals fell manna-like upon their communities. Jim Baker, master delegate cowpuncher, rounded up practically all of the Pennsylvania strays for President Ford. Reagan ended up having traded his number-one chit, the Vice Presidency, for a total of four delegates.

For Reagan that meant the end of the line. The nomination belonged to Ford. For Jim Baker, it meant a battlefield promotion: overall charge of Ford's fall campaign.

This was only a prelude to the ultimate test of wits between Reagan and Baker, who materialized in the next Presidential campaign as manager for his old friend George Bush, with the top priority of saving America from "voodoo economics," apparently not a priority shared by the American voter—not the *Republican* voter, certainly. After an upset victory in the Iowa caucuses, the Bush campaign's "Big Mo" quickly fizzled. "Bush for President" placards were replaced by "Bush for Vice President" placards, and his manager began a quiet metamorphosis which would transform him in a few weeks from loser's campaign manager to winner's top adviser, from caterpillar to butterfly.

By putting Baker in the staff chief's job, Reagan demonstrated that important rule of power: *Keep your enemies in front of you.* A shrewd politician does not banish his adversaries but follows the more primitive custom of taking hostages.

The appointment of Jim Baker was as much a triumph for the new President as it was for his first White House chief of staff. The crusading outsider had co-opted a prince of the powers-that-be, with close ties to the remnants of the party's Eastern establishment and to the national press corps.

Jim Baker, who went on to become Secretary of the Treasury, will be remembered as a superb packager of Reagan's legislative plan, smoothing his West Wing colleagues' rough ideological edges and winning respect from the Washington media. To the congressional opposition, he was a courtly professional, the "good cop" in the Reagan White House. Many a potential irritation was avoided by a respectful and confidential drop-in at the Speaker's office. To reporters, Baker was the "White House pragmatist," someone who would give it to them straight.

In each respect, Baker's abilities would shine far brighter in the later years of the Reagan administration, when his absence from the White House became painfully evident. As the smart politics and close-order drill of the first Reagan administration gave way to the dementia and chaos of the second, Jim Baker's was the name uttered with the intensest longing. The poison of the Iran affair would never have seeped under the West Wing door had he still been in the building.

Reagan's initial master stroke was not simply in hiring Jim Baker but in putting his old adversary in a position where he could not do well unless his President did well. In the West Wing, intercom distance from the President, Baker's success would be measured entirely in terms of Reagan's own accomplishments. Had he started out with his own department or agency, Baker would have had the opportunity to create his own fiefdom, to establish a separate reputation and constituency. The newspaper profiles of Baker might have been headlined "The One Bright Light in the Reagan Cabinet" while the President's own agenda died in gridlock. As chief of staff, Baker was fully leveraged. Baker's achievements could only enhance his boss's; he had no choice but to make the Reagan Revolution a winner.

The idea of bringing old rivals into a new Administration did not begin with Reagan. Franklin D. Roosevelt defeated Wendell L. Willkie in the 1940 election, then made him special envoy to Britain a few months later. The purpose was clear: Willkie had attacked Roosevelt's close support of Britain during the campaign; now he was being used to reassert a bipartisan thrust to FDR's policies. Later in the decade, Harry Truman commissioned former President Herbert Hoover to oversee a complete review of the federal organizational structure. In tapping Hoover's acute managerial and engineering ability, the Democratic President was also giving his Administration some needed credibility on the growing "waste and corruption" issue.

Yet it was Abraham Lincoln, operating under far more demanding circumstances, who made an art of co-opting his adversaries. Imagine the predicament the great man confronted. Threats to his life were so rampant in 1861 that he and his family had to enter the capital in secret. The military situation was even more dreadful. When he arrived in Washington, Lincoln could look across the Potomac River and see the Confederate flag flying over the port of Alexandria.

Even in the loyal states trouble ran deep. The first Republican President led a brand-new party composed of two conflicting elements: the radical abolitionists, who shared the spirit if not the tactics of John Brown, and what remained of the old Whigs. Before Lincoln could save the Union, he first had to weld together his own political factions.

Rather than assemble his entire Administration from among his own dedicated followers, the President-elect resolved to bring his enemies aboard. He put together a government by yoking together the fanatical Salmon P. Chase and the cautious William H. Seward, and brought forth a Cabinet said to be united on only two points: they all hated one another, and each member thought he would make a better President than Abraham Lincoln.

"They will eat you up," the President was warned. "They will be just as likely to eat each other up," he replied with an old hand's detachment. He was shrewd, and tough enough to recruit strong men and put them into the right positions under his controlling eye. He was certain of success only when Seward and Chase both resigned and he kept them on, their letters of resignation now both in his safekeeping. "I have a melon in each corner of my sack," he said.

In the Carter Administration, I saw how making sure the new recruit's hopes being pinned to the top man's success is as critical as the recruitment itself. Without it, the skipper finds himself with a loose cannon on deck.

When Jimmy Carter became President in 1977, one department, Health, Education and Welfare, had a budget greater than those of all of the fifty states put together and larger than that of any other country in the world but the Soviet Union. In accepting the appointment as Secretary of HEW, Joseph A. Califano also accepted a more personal assignment: in his own words, "the boundless challenge of the Secretary's job was to promote social justice and to persuade, educate, cajole, and plead with the people, the Congress, the public servants at HEW, and often a President and administration besieged by crises and other demands, here and abroad."

Califano's understanding of his new post as a platform for the independent advocacy of progressive action was consistent with President Carter's decision to hire him in the first place. Carter wanted on his team a representative of the liberal Democratic establishment. He had run against that establishment and defeated it. Now it was time to share some of the power and patronage of office. According to aide Jody Powell, the newly elected President also wanted someone who "knew the game in Washington and how to play." Carter had his own agenda of reform—welfare, health insurance—and he needed someone who could keep all the balls in the air without having his own cut off.

In this light, the appointment of so proven a Washington gladiator as Califano made perfect sense. Since serving as Lyndon Johnson's dynamic staff chief, Califano had become a key Washington figure. Counsel to both the Democratic National Committee and the *Washington Post*, he was the classic insider, with a list of friends that defined all elements of power in the city: Congress, the major law firms, the media, and the veterans of past Democratic Administrations who had long since made Washington their permanent home and power base.

The new President obviously hoped to win these constituencies' goodwill by giving them one of their own to run the Great Society programs that so many of them—Califano, most of all—had helped create. But Carter never reckoned with the politics of the new relationship, how he would control the hardballer he had just recruited to his team.

In selecting Califano, the President knew he was getting an advocate of strong government action. While Califano shared Carter's determination to make his department's programs more efficient, he retained an un-Carter-like passion that those programs fully address their initial objectives. On matters of civil-rights enforcement, health and education there would be no compromise of progressive ideals.

It soon became apparent that this highly aggressive approach would exact political costs from the new Administration. In North Carolina, for example, Califano vigorously and hotly pursued an anti-discrimination case against the state's beloved university system, while tobacco farmers felt the full brunt of his campaign against cigarette smoking. Both actions were highly defensible. Califano had a federal judge threatening to hold him in contempt if he wavered on the UNC matter. With 300,000 smokers dying each year of lung and other diseases, he had become a zealous convert to the anti-tobacco issue.

Facing the dim prospect of winning reelection without North Carolina or Kentucky, a state whose governor was calling for Califano's scalp, Carter and his White House staff became uneasy. The Secretary continued to move ahead. Yet, with the thermometer rising in the West Wing, the President never told him to yield on the antismoking crusade. The more the *New York Times* liked Califano, the more embittered the small-town North Carolina and Kentucky newspapers grew toward Carter.

The distance between President and appointee attained absurd proportions when, in the wake of Califano's high-profile campaign, Carter desperately told a North Carolina audience of his desire "to make the smoking of tobacco even more safe than it is today."

A second area of dispute grew over Carter's commitment to the creation of a separate Department of Education. Califano spent the first year of the Administration arguing forthrightly against the idea on the grounds that the new agency would be responsive to political pressure from teachers' unions and not to broad objectives. Carter, though willing to give the matter more study, never ceased in his desire to meet what he and the National Education Association viewed as a deeply personal commitment. By the time Carter made the proposal formal, in his 1978 State of the Union Message, everyone who cared about the issue knew that the President was fulfilling a promise that his own Secretary openly considered a terrible idea. Thanks to Califano, they also knew the full and varied hazards of the Carter plan.

How could such intramural chaos invade an Administration pledged to improving government efficiency? First, there was the whole premise of Califano's appointment. In the initial, pre-appointment interview, the President-elect had said, "I intend to keep my promise of Cabinet government to the American people." His Secretaries would pick their own people, run their own departments. In the case of Califano and HEW, the Cabinet member insisted on his complete right to make whatever departmental appointments he wanted, notwithstanding the view from the White House.

That, Jody Powell admitted later, may have been the fatal error. "My impression is that he'll push and push until he meets resistance," he said of Califano. As time went on, it became harder and harder for the Carter people to resist. "It became harder to rein him in," Powell recalled. "Not only was Carter weaker, but it was harder to take back what Califano already thought he had." This was the White House view. As far as his HEW Secretary was concerned, Carter "didn't run the government" to begin with.

Carter's mistake was in suggesting that any Cabinet secretary should be, *could* be, independent of the President who appoints him. Unlike judges, executive-branch appointees serve *at the pleasure of the President*. The public knows that and holds the Chief Executive responsible. Whatever the program or policy, the buck stops with one man, the one they elected.

Califano believed otherwise. "It goes with the territory for a Cabinet officer to put a little distance between himself and the President," he has written. It allows the Chief Executive to "shield" himself on sensitive issues. Yet in the case of his campaign against smoking and his opposition to a department of education, Califano ran counter to the President's immediate political ambitions. There had been a serious mishandling of the relationship. It ended with the President asking for his HEW Secretary's resignation in 1979.

What stands out here is the timing. It would be hard to imagine Lyndon Johnson or Ronald Reagan permitting a subordinate to publicly carry out policies that were out of step with the Presidential agenda. Facing re-election, it is hard to imagine them not making anyone they appointed damned aware that the President might yank their chair any minute they were on the job. Regardless of what had been said up front about their being "free to run their own departments." More to the point, if someone in LBJ's time had tried to play hardball with the President, the White House chief of staff—Joe Califano, that is—would have recommended that his boss show the underling how the game is played!

Jimmy Carter ignored the "Keep your enemies in front of you" rule and paid for it. Like most people, he was inclined to keep potential adversaries at arm's length. The result was crippling. Having defeated the Democratic establishment on his way to the Oval Office, Carter soon found that same establishment standing smugly on the sidelines, rooting for his downfall. His Administration found itself cut off, not only from the emerging American right, but also from the forces that usually accommodate a Democratic Presidency.

Observe the contrast. Reagan put Jim Baker into a position where his interests had to coincide with the whole Administration's; Carter gave Califano the independence to build a seceding empire. Instead of subjecting him to the limits necessary to handle so proven and headstrong a man in partnership with so well-connected a bureaucracy, Carter gave him free rein, allowing a situation to develop in which Califano would respond only to direct order from the President.

History is partially to blame. To avoid the creation of another Nixon-style "palace guard" at the White House, Carter made it clear up front that he didn't want his staff directing the Cabinet. The result: he deprived himself of day-to-day regulation of his own executive departments short of an in-person Presidential investigation and command. Since situations often develop where the President cannot permit himself to get involved personally, this creates a giant power vacuum.

At one point, in February of 1978, the White House aide responsible for liaison with the various departments, Jack Watson, called Califano to tell him of the political dangers President Carter was facing in North Carolina. He said the antismoking campaign, together with the HEW move against the North Carolina university system, could cost Carter the state in the next election. And he said that the President wanted to talk to him about the matter.

A few days later, in early March, Vice President Mondale invited Califano to lunch. When he tried to bring up the antismoking campaign, the Secretary cut him short. Califano warned him that he could not vouch for the confidentiality of such a discussion. He said that the press had been asking him whether the White House had contacted him with regard to the campaign and that he had been able to deny it "so far." Hearing this, Mondale retreated.

Carter was boxed into a powerless position. He was being told by one of his own Cabinet Secretaries that anything he said on a controversial subject like tobacco could be used against him. He was unable to call Califano off the antismoking campaign without being publicly embarrassed in the press. Califano, meanwhile, assumed the position that he could take the President's personal silence for consent. If Carter didn't personally give him a direct order, he could continue with his own, departmental agenda.

When recruiting his Cabinet in late 1976, Jimmy Carter never contemplated dealing with a hardballer like Califano. He was still trying to avoid another Watergate. To avoid the arrogant and dangerous concentration of power in the Nixon White House, where Chief-of-staff H.R. "Bob" Haldeman held a dangerous level of authority, Jimmy Carter had gone to another extreme. His governing principle seemed to be "Let a thousand flowers bloom."

In hiring Califano, Carter observed the same axiom that Lyndon Johnson had cited in retaining FBI Director J. Edgar Hoover in office, "Better to have them inside the tent pissin' out than outside pissin' in."

But the Georgian had ignored the great Texan's corollary, "Hug your friends tight, but your enemies tighter—hug 'em so tight they can't wiggle."

This lesson counts in all professions. If you want to hire the best people in any line of activity, check out those working for your fiercest competition. Talent is talent, and no matter how hot the rivalry, never forget that you are likely to need the other guy's help someday. It would be surprising, in fact, if you can't do some business with him somewhere down the road. Besides, hiring your rivals

shows nerve. It not only builds your reputation and resolution but frequently weakens theirs.

Our first impulses prod us, of course, to avoid those who
act against us. Life is short, after all. Who needs the hassle?
Such an attitude is fine for those whose number-one objective is to make their days as pleasant and stress-free as
possible. It's also a prescription for avoiding power, not
acquiring it.

A businessman who fails to meet with his rivals throws
away golden opportunities not just for useful scuttlebutt
but for useful contacts. Being ill at ease in a rival's company doesn't just put a big crimp in your style: it's hard to
deal if you're not even at the table!

The strong leader rejects the path of least resistance.
Rather than shun opponents—"I'm not speaking to those
fellas"—he co-opts them, thus keeping tabs on what
they're up to, gauging their emotions and generally intimidating them. Ted Sorensen saw Jack Kennedy do this to
his political critics. "When someone was knocking him, he
always let him know that *he* knew."

He did not have to teach this rule to Tip O'Neill.

I was present at a memorable demonstration of the unsettling "Keep your enemies in front of you" ploy in 1984.
The scene was the Speaker's office at the beginning of his
daily press conference. Ensconced as always in his huge
swivel chair, O'Neill was sitting with the rest of the Democratic leadership waiting for the Capitol press corps to
rush through the door.

The Democratic Party was then in particular turmoil.
Walter Mondale, who had the Speaker's complete trust
and support, was headed toward crushing defeat in his
battle to unseat President Reagan. Innumerable congressional seats appeared to be in jeopardy. There were even
faint rumblings of a possible leadership challenge within
the House.

One of those mentioned as a challenger to the Speaker was now sitting just a few feet away. We could hear the press rushing through the door to the Speaker's rooms when O'Neill swung round and demanded, "Are you running against me?"

It was a punch to the solar plexus. "No," the stricken pretender mumbled. "No, I'm not running."

Mission accomplished.

Chapter Six

Don't Get Mad; Don't Get Even; Get Ahead

I always throw my golf club in the direction I'm going.
—RONALD REAGAN

Revenge is the nitroglycerin of politics. *In extremis,* it can get the heart started again. Used improperly, it can blow your head off.

Despite a reputation for endless intrigue, smart politicians prefer to co-opt their enemies. When this proves impossible, they move with the same cold resolve with which they strike alliances, defeating adversaries not by flailing blindly but by concentrating their own forces. Rather than a desperate charge "over the top," they dig the trenches deeper, work their networks wider. Rather than trying to weaken their opponents, they strengthen themselves. Inevitably, those most intent on reaching their own goals gain a valuable byproduct: a greater capacity to render justice. Like Ronald Reagan, the infrequent golfer, they keep their eyes on the ball, their minds on their destination. When angered, they throw their golf clubs in the same direction they're headed, so that they can retrieve them on the way to the hole.

As we will see, it's better to get even than to get mad, but better still to get ahead.

Among his friends, Francis Patrick Sullivan was some-

107

thing of a legend in this department. Like the insane pro-
tagonist in Edgar Allan Poe's "The Casque of Amontil-
lado," he tolerated injury, but when his adversary turned
to insult he vowed revenge.

For years, Sully's ambition had been to land a big job on
Capitol Hill. His problem was the method he chose. He
thought that if he could just meet congressmen after hours,
gathering with lobbyists at those little nightspots clustered
round the Hill, he could charm them with his blarney.

There was a hitch in the strategy. Professionals like to
keep their private and office lives separate. They don't go
drinking with their staffs. They don't hire people they met
in some smoke-filled gin mill the night before. After sharing a few beers with Sully at some seedy Hill-side joint,
the honorable member was slow to reach for Sully's call-
back slips in the harsh light of day. And Sully had another
handicap: he carried a grudge, a big one, never more than
two drinks from the surface.

Back in 1974, his big chance for glory on the Hill had
finally arrived. He was managing a House campaign just
across the Potomac and making the most of it. By election
day, he had raised $80,000 and recruited some two thou-
sand volunteers. His battle cry to the recruits was relentless and joyous. "Dare to be great," he would yell to one
and all. "Let's win this one for Herbie."

Now, even Sully would admit, *sotto voce,* that "Herbie"
was no great shakes. But, let's face it, it wasn't the cut of
the man's jib that intrigued Sully, but his prospects. Surely
Sully had himself a winner this time.

And "Herbie" turned out to be, at least electorally, a
winner. Watergate gave him what had been a Republican
seat. Then, the morning after the election, the ax fell. Pat
Sullivan was told with the minimum of consideration that
he wasn't "cut out" for work in a congressional office. The
victorious candidate, the man he thought was his patron,

said that he would have to help Sully find "something else."

Sully did not take the news well. The rejection by a man he did not much respect to begin with knocked him off balance for a long time. He spent a couple of years drinking, telling everyone that he hated "Herbie's" guts. As the months passed, he carried his frustrations to ridiculous extremes, at one point sending a Christmas card to the new Congressman, with a note saying that he was "enjoying his third month of unemployment."

For a long time, Sully was like many people you meet in politics, their lives obsessively focused on a single bad break. Sully went further. If "Herbie" had a fund-raiser, his old campaign manager would organize some sort of demonstration to disrupt it. He even switched political parties. Elections and candidates would come and go, but his presence in the Republican camp was a certainty.

Finally, after six years, Sully saw his chance. Reading through the local weekly, he came upon an advertisement for a fringe candidate for U.S. Congress running against Herbie. For Pat Sullivan, the long, dreary march was coming to an end.

The candidate's cause was the liberalization of marijuana laws. Sully offered his expertise. It was not the issue that mattered, but the cause. Here was a candidate who would attract votes from the young, single people who lived in the district's high-rise apartments.

It was 1980, a year when larger issues loomed in the land, but Sully knew his district. There would be thousands of people who usually voted for the liberal Democrat but who would just as soon throw their vote to a colorful anti-establishment type.

Without his help, the "marijuana candidate" would not have been what politicians call a "factor." She knew nothing of politics. When Sully found her, she was collecting signatures for her filing petition from voters outside the district!

Her new ally made her candidacy a reality. She won a spot on the ballot, and she garnered six thousand votes—not enough to win, but just enough to doom "Herbie," who lost to someone else by ninety-four votes. But Sully had yet to drive the last nail into the coffin.

When the next congressional election came around and with it "Herbie's" anticipated comeback bid, Sully was there to administer the *coup de grâce*.

Other things being equal, it should have been a good year for a Democrat. The country was plunging into recession. The President was being attacked for tampering with Social Security. In most parts of the United States the results reflected the voters' mood, and the Democrats picked up twenty-six House seats. Unfortunately for "Herbie," his old district was not among them. His nemesis had again found himself a spoiler to skim off the youthful, liberal votes that the Democrats consider theirs.

Keeping up with current tastes, Sully this time found an antinuclear activist, a real earth-shoe-wearing, whale-saving one-worlder. Sully's new pawn wasn't as successful as the pro-drug candidate—he won only three thousand votes —but he did well enough to cost "Herbie" the race by five hundred votes. The earth pattered down on "Herbie's" coffin lid.

To the very end, Sullivan's increasingly desperate ingrate tried to deny what was happening to him. Only on election eve did the strain become too much. With polling a mere few days away, "Herbie" was invited to participate in a debate sponsored by an important civic group. To his dismay, he arrived to find that it was a three-way debate: he, the Republican Congressman (whom "Herbie" had beaten eight years earlier with Sully's help) and Sully's antinuker.

"I demand to know if Pat Sullivan is working for you," shrieked "Herbie." "If he is, you're sick!"

But Sully's mission was close to accomplished: the political eradication of his betrayer. On election night 1982, when other Democrats in the country were basking in victory, Sully penned one last letter to his victim:

"Dear Former Congressman . . ."

There is a downside to the story of F. Patrick Sullivan's revenge. Though he has harpooned his great white whale and put his drinking behind him, Sully is the first to admit the all-too-measurable damage to himself. "Herbie lived rent-free in my head for eight years," he later said.

Sully's story shows the pains to which people will go for vengeance, sadly paralleling the genius we see in those great criminal minds whose schemes to rob banks so often exceed in originality the planning of those who own them.

Ask anyone in a congressional cloakroom what he thinks of the old "Don't get mad; get even" line (it is traceable to Illinois Senator Everett M. Dirksen) and you get the same hard-bitten assessment: "Not worth it." "Too expensive." "Waste of time." "Takes too damned long." As Maryland's former Governor Marvin Mandel put it, "Don't spend your life looking through a rearview mirror."

Dan Rostenkowski of Illinois, chairman of the powerful House Ways and Means Committee, is the victim of a little fellow with a mighty memory. In 1968 Rosty was on his way to becoming Speaker. He was only forty but already had a decade's seniority and a secure seat from Chicago's North Side. A political hot property, "one of the boys," he was the kind of congressman who moves upward as by a law of nature.

Rostenkowski's express lane to the Speaker's chair hit a major detour in 1968 when the Democrats went to Chicago for that summer's infamous national convention. Vietnam was dominating the country's attention. Outside, in Grant

Park and on the streets, students were rallying to the anti-war cause. The Chicago police were bashing their brains in.

Inside Convention Hall, Mayor Richard J. Daley, the "Boss," was trying to act as if nothing were happening. His business was politics, not foreign policy. He was concerned that the proceedings reflect well on the city.

He never counted on the impact of television. No police-shielded hall could be insulated from the violence in the streets. Delegates began to raise their voices against Daley and his harsh methods. Senator Abraham A. Ribicoff of Connecticut stood at the podium and condemned "Gestapo tactics in the streets of Chicago."

At this point, the mayor and a phalanx of his people down on the floor began yelling. With the chaos outside now filtering into the hall like tear gas through a wet handkerchief, Daley tried to scream Ribicoff down, running his hand hard across his neck in the cut-'em-off gesture. His televised lips, analyzed later, distilled the Boss's views in all their ethnic rage: "Fuck you, you Jew sonofabitch! You lousy motherfucker! Go home!"

Hizzoner was not the only man infuriated by what he saw. Watching the carnage on television, Lyndon Johnson put through a call from the White House. It was clear that the convention's dwarfish chairman, House Majority Leader Carl Albert of Oklahoma, was not the man to restore order. The lame-duck President wanted someone tougher wielding the gavel.

Rosty remembers the phone call well. "He started screaming his head off at me." The President wanted him to *do something*. Passing a sanitized version of the word to Albert, Rostenkowski assumed the chair. The price would be a much more coveted chair.

Three years later, Albert became Speaker of the House and took his revenge. When the new Majority Leader,

Hale Boggs of Louisiana, recommended Rostenkowski as whip, the party's third-ranking position, Speaker Albert turned him down cold, despite the fact that Rosty was the next man in line. He put the call through to Tip O'Neill instead.

Albert was not finished with Rosty. A few days later, Rostenkowski ran for reelection to his job as chairman of the House Democratic Caucus and was rolled over by a surprise late entrant into the race: Olin E. "Tiger" Teague of Texas, Carl Albert's candidate.

That's how Dan Rostenkowski lost his position on the House leadership ladder. Thinking back on that memorable moment at the '68 convention years later, one friend of the Illinois Congressman muttered, "Danny would be Speaker right now if he had kept his mouth shut."

Observing the "get ahead" rule, some others have scored far higher. Consider one case where a personal slight, handled professionally, became a spur to advancement.

In 1948, Democrat Chester Bowles, like the head of the ticket, Harry Truman, came from behind to win Democratic, in his case the governorship of Connecticut. No one was more thrilled than his state chairman, John Bailey. The candidate had run the election just the way Bailey had planned, and that night an exhausted chairman said, "It's something I've worked for for two years."

Victory was to be followed by humiliation. The following year, one of Connecticut's U.S. senators resigned. Bailey made known his interest in being appointed to the vacancy. All he wanted was to have the seat until the election was held in 1950. He would gladly step aside when it came time to select the candidate; he sought the honor, not the career. Bailey's claims on the governor's gratitude were immense; nevertheless Bowles chose William Benton, who had made a fortune as Bowles's partner in the advertising business and who could trace his family to the *Mayflower*—but who had done nothing for the Connecticut Democratic Party.

Bailey, an Irish Catholic, was deeply upset at the governor's rebuff but refused to let his disappointment show. Years later he said, "I guess he was worried about what the people out in Michigan and Washington would think about him appointing a small-time politician to the U.S. Senate." Though it was presumed he had the power to deny Bowles renomination, Bailey did not want to hurt the party he had built. Instead, he went to work making peace, quelling the opposition to Benton's appointment among party regulars. When the new Senator visited Hartford, Bailey invited him to stay at his home, a practice that he continued thereafter. The two families became friends.

In 1954, the time came again for Connecticut Democrats to pick a candidate for governor. Bowles, who had been defeated for a four-year term in 1950, was seeking a comeback. Chairman Bailey toured the state, asking party officials to record their preference by dropping a ballot into a black shoebox he carried with him. Finally, Bailey signaled his choice: Abe Ribicoff. Asked about the ballots years later, Bailey simply said, "Oh, Abe had a lot of votes." Ribicoff went on to a smashing political career as governor, Cabinet secretary and U.S. senator. What he may have lacked in Pilgrim ancestry he made up for with a certain Irishman's friendship.

Four years later, Bowles attempted one last race and was defeated for the Senate, this time by Thomas J. Dodd, whose campaign went over the top with the convention vote of a fresh new ally of Bailey's, Mrs. Ella Grasso. As a liberal, the future governor would have been expected to go with Bowles. Her vote for Dodd let everyone know, once and for all, where the party chairman stood. Three years later, in 1961 John Bailey moved to Washington with the new President, John F. Kennedy, as chairman of the Democratic National Committee.

Asked about the effect of his early setback, those close to Bailey say that losing that Senate seat was the best thing that ever happened to him. "If he had received that honor in the 1940s, he would have quit," one relative now says. "Instead, he set a higher goal and it gave purpose to his whole life."

Rule: Always keep your eye on the goal. *Accumulate power, and the opportunities to render justice will fall onto your plate.* It takes brains and, most important, time.

John Bailey, who was too fine a man to ever engage in single-minded vengeance, has a lesson to teach on how to deal with an adversary. Rather than be diminished by the slight, he was raised by it. Instead of bad-mouthing his rival, he simply outdistanced and outgrew him. Jack Kennedy also knew the difference between political justice and peevishness. When he ran for office the first time, he carried a looseleaf book of quotations around with him. One of them was from his father. "More men die of jealousy than of cancer," it read.

The son learned from the father's hard-won wisdom. "He would reward his opponents," Ted Sorensen recalls with irony, "but he would never forget which department store wouldn't put his posters in its windows back in '48."

Kennedy's successor in Congress, Tip O'Neill, was of the same school. In 1980, a wealthy socialite named John LeBoutillier was elected to the Congress to represent the *Great Gatsby* area of Long Island, New York. He won with the help of two considerable assets: the full backing of the local Republican machine, and a sizable campaign war chest (his Vanderbilt and Whitney relatives had pitched in grandly). LeBoutillier seemed headed toward a substantial career.

But early in his tenure he made a wee mistake. He gave

a speech at a New York Republican state convention in which he said that House Speaker Thomas P. O'Neill was "fat, bloated and out of control—just like the federal budget." It was a Saturday, always a slow day for news. The wires picked it up. Bob Schieffer read it on *CBS News*.

Many people were indignant at the contempt shown for the Speaker, his office and for the House of Representatives over which he presides. The Speaker himself had little to say. When he was asked what he thought of the man who had so viciously lampooned him, his words were dry and cold: "I wouldn't know him from a cord of wood."

Two years later, Democrats were holding a fund-raiser to "roast" Tip O'Neill. One of the speakers was Congressman Robert J. Mrazek, who had defeated LeBoutillier in the recently-held election. "For a while there, I had no idea where we would get the money we needed to run a decent campaign," he said. "Then, out of nowhere, three weeks before election day, the money started pouring in, from Chicago, from everywhere." Many of these contributors had obviously never heard of Bob Mrazek. They didn't know him from a cord of wood. They just wanted to shut an impudent mouth.

Some time thereafter, a certain rich young man found himself dining in a Washington restaurant. Seeing the Speaker at another table, he sent over a bottle of wine and a few minutes later came over himself. "I just wanted to say hello," he said. "I'm John LeBoutillier. I guess you were more popular than I thought you were."

Chapter Seven

Leave No Shot Unanswered

> If you don't have something good to say about
> someone, come sit next to me.
> —ALICE ROOSEVELT LONGWORTH

It's easy to keep track of Claude Pepper's age. He was born in 1900, just nine months into the century. The oldest member of the U.S. Congress, he also had some of the best stories to tell. Unfortunately for Pepper, his most startling tale was a lesson he learned the hard way. He is one politician who discovered to his lasting regret the folly of letting false shots go unanswered.

Most people have come to know Pepper as a late-in-life crusader for the nation's senior citizens. His is the familiar, weathered face we see at Grey Panther rallies, excoriating anyone who dares think of tampering with Social Security. An aide to President Reagan once commented to *Time* that there are only two people who really get under Reagan's skin, "Tip O'Neill and that Congressman from Florida who keeps talking about Social Security."

I remember standing at a reception in 1982 for the newly elected members of the House. As the bright-eyed new representatives and their spouses hobnobbed and rubbernecked their way around the Capitol's Rayburn Room, some paused to listen to the one member greeting them who had served in the U.S. Congress back in the years before Rayburn was even Speaker. Claude Pepper was telling a new member from Long Island about the efforts to bring America into World War II. He spoke from experience. It was the "Pepper Resolution" that compromised U.S. neutrality and allowed our country to provide direct aid to Great Britain.

Claude Pepper's career in the House spans three decades. Actually he is now in his second career in the Congress, a sequel to a political lifetime that began in the New Deal days of 1936 and ended with apparent finality in 1950 when Pepper lost his Senate seat. He is still called "Senator Pepper" by his staff and colleagues.

A lot of politicians look back at the 1950 Senate Democratic primary in Florida as the dirtiest in history. This was the infamous "Red Pepper" campaign, in which the incumbent Senator was painted as a dupe of Stalin and an enemy of free enterprise. Nor did the attack stop with red-baiting. Absurd but sinister-sounding charges—"Pepper is known all over Washington as a shameless *extrovert!*" "Pepper has a sister who was once a *thespian!*" "Pepper practiced *celibacy* before his marriage!"—were pumped into the cracker back country.

That year, seven U.S. senators were defeated for reelection. None of them seemed even remotely prepared for the paintbrush that would leave them crimson red, their careers and reputations devastated. Pepper, the first of them to go down—he lost in a May primary—had refused to fire back. That is one of the things he remembers most vividly. He was the first victim of the red-baiting and the one least prepared.

Sitting in his chandeliered office on the third floor of the Capitol, Pepper told me about the "Red Pepper campaign." He recalled his adversary, George A. Smathers, and the tactics he used. And he reworked what his response should have been to the charges. "I've thought very often about that campaign and what I could have done," he said thirty-six years later like Sherlock Holmes still trying to crack an old and difficult case.

Part of the problem was timing. It was the first use in a party primary of what would be called McCarthyism. All the other senators defeated that year were challenged in the general election. The "Red Pepper" campaign would serve, in fact, as a model for these later debacles.

Pepper's opponent was another surprise. George Smathers had managed Pepper's 1938 campaign. Afterward Pepper had helped him become assistant U.S. attorney for the district. Then, in 1945, Pepper had asked Attorney General Tom Clark to make Smathers one of his assistants, an appointment that won him early discharge from the Marine Corps.

Smathers' campaign for this second appointment was not one of the things he would brag about. Pepper remembers how the younger man had come to him in June 1945, with World War II still raging in the Pacific. "For three weeks he importuned me. He wanted to get out of the service so that Tom Clark could make him an assistant attorney general. When Smathers finally succeeded in getting his discharge, his mother wrote, 'Thank God for men like Claude Pepper.' "

Pepper's role as Smathers' mentor did not end there. When Smathers ran for Congress in 1946, he was characterized by the conservative opposition as "the Pepper candidate." When he asked the Senator how to handle the charge, Pepper advised his young colleague to say, "They're trying to throw pepper in folks' eyes." Smathers eagerly took the advice.

While Pepper was pushing Smathers' career, the state's powerful business interests, increasingly angered by the Senator's support for minimum-wage legislation and national health insurance and his opposition to a Republican tax-relief bill, were amassing a huge campaign war chest

to defeat Pepper for renomination in 1950, and they found
the man to spend it on: George Smathers.

Smathers went immediately on the attack. Announcing
his candidacy in January, he said he "would not tolerate
traitors." The implication was overpowering. He was red-
baiting his patron, the man who had helped build his career.

Pepper failed to deflect the personal attacks. "They
caught me by surprise," he says almost four decades later.
"I never dreamed of the nature of the campaign, the *per-
suasiveness* of it." Even after he began his own campaign
two months before the primary, he failed to recognize the
damage being done. "I still didn't realize the magnitude
of the thing."

Eventually, Pepper himself was unwittingly made an
accomplice in the dirty-tricks campaign. In the South at
that time, there existed an ultimate weapon—and it was
only a question of how and when it would be armed and
detonated.

One night in Leesburg, after the Senator had completed
a speech and was stepping down from an outdoor platform
his supporters had built, he was approached by a man who
reached out to clasp his hand. The picture filled a half page
in the next day's *Orlando Sentinel*, for the man was black.
In segregationist Florida, the picture of a major white politician glad-handing for black support was a political death
warrant. "That *hurt*," Pepper recalls. Only later would af-
fidavits confirm that the man, a janitor at a local theater,
had been paid to stand there, grab the Senator's hand
when he came down, and hold it "until the light flashes."

But it was the Bolshevik charge that cut deepest. On
Sunday, three days before the primary, the incumbent felt
its full enormity. As he came out of church, a woman
showed him a pamphlet she had just been handed that
morning. Its title was "The Red Record of Senator Pep-

per." In the hours that followed, tens of thousands of these booklets were trucked throughout the state. By the time the Pepper campaign realized what had happened, it was too late to do anything about it.

Looking back, Pepper believes that his whole strategy had been flawed, that his campaign "made every mistake in the book."

The first was to let the charges against him pass unchallenged. "I had always followed the rule of not mentioning my opponent's name. I would always run on the theory I was applying for a job. I would always tell the people what I thought I was qualified to do and not mention the other applicants." The problem with speaking-no-evil was that people were getting some far more lurid information on Pepper from his enemies. By refusing to counter the charges or attack the credibility of those making them, he gave his longtime supporters the wrong idea.

Pepper now realizes that his best tactic would have been to start early and hit Smathers with everything he had. When his opponent leveled the "traitor" charge, he should have hit his former protégé as a liar and an ingrate. "I should have said, 'If he'll doublecross a friend, he'll doublecross you.' " Pepper believes that he could have destroyed Smathers' credibility had he released the story of his superpatriot challenger's shameless efforts to win release from the Marines so that he could get a head start in postwar politics.

If the Senator had fought back with any degree of ferocity, the "Red Pepper" campaign might have lost its bite. Instead, the campaign became a model, especially for an ambitious candidate at the other end of the continent.

In the later months of 1950, it became clear that a young California congressman had studied the Smathers campaign in some detail. Richard Nixon dubbed his opponent, Representative Helen Gahagan Douglas, the "pink lady."

Nixon's agents printed a campaign leaflet pairing Douglas' voting record with that of the radical Congressman Vito Marcantonio of New York City. Years later, the document known as the "pink sheet" made Nixon the pariah of the nation's liberals. But as in Florida six months earlier, the charges stuck. Thus began Nixon's Senate career.

When someone makes an unfair attack, the onus is on the victim to set the record straight. In these days of twenty-four-hour Cable News Network broadcasting, a damaging wire story can be on the air within the hour. Any story, particularly a negative one, travels at the speed of light, creating an electronic paperstorm flying in every direction. A sad rule of thumb is that most people believe that if any shot goes unanswered it must be true.

Fortunately, there are as many good defenses as there are good offenses. With daring and a good bit of humor you can leave your critic wishing he had kept his powder dry.

METHOD NO. 1: CATCH 'EM IN A LIE.

Some of the most memorable campaigns in history have been won by the victims of slanders. In each case, what swept the election was the successful counterattack, the cleverness in calling "Foul!"

In 1970, Senator Frank Moss of Utah was charged by his Republican opponent with supporting violent demonstrations by students against the war in Vietnam. Moss destroyed the man by running full-page newspaper ads displaying a letter he had sent to the young demonstrators supporting their objective but urging them to avoid violence. Across the top of the page the headline read: "Here's the Famous Letter." It won the election.

Another case in point was the 1982 senatorial campaign in New York.

Earlier that year, the electoral prospects of the incumbent, Daniel Patrick Moynihan, were not promising. The Republicans, fresh from their 1980 landslide, were planning to nominate an extremely attractive young opponent who had made a reputation in the House of Representatives as a tough critic of the liberal establishment, Speaker O'Neill in particular. Disrespectful of seniority, this young Republican firebrand seemed to relish hitting those who were highest on the political ladder. They made good targets for a political gunslinger trying to make his mark.

Moynihan, the erudite academic, was the best target of all. His inflection came from Harvard Yard, his liberalism from Hell's Kitchen. To Republicans, he was the worst of all worlds: liberal, intellectual, and a big-city Democrat ever alert to his party's demanding constituencies.

But Moynihan did have certain political assets. One of them was his chief of staff and press secretary, Timothy Russert, who recognized that an effective way to counter one assertion, in this case that the Senator was too soft toward the Soviets, was to catch him lying in another. Scouting the opposition for the '82 campaign, Russert began noticing that the hotshot Republican challenger, so schooled in political attack, was a little fuzzy defining his own past. The problem revolved around his war record.

Certain discrepancies began to surface in the young hero's account of his service. As a congressional candidate in the late 1970s, he had emphasized his desk jockey job at the Pentagon as a whiz-kid planner in the nation's conversion to a peacetime economy. Identifying with the post-Vietnam transition, he seemed to be making himself an agent in the winding down of the war itself.

In the more hawkish 1980s, a different color began to glow in the self-portrait. Now the nation was reeling from the Iranian hostage-taking. The country was in a *Rambo* mood, and the young "veteran" was riding the Zeitgeist. Suddenly his literature began portraying him not as a Pentagon pencil pusher but as a real-life soldier, who might actually have gotten his hands dirty in 'Nam.

Russert began sorting through the candidate's speeches, press releases and news clips. Working with a yellow legal pad, he systematically marked down every fact put out about the other fellow's record until a blatant pattern emerged. The Pentagon intellectual had been purely a paper John Wayne. The truth was actually closer to the earlier portrait. Far from being a commissioned officer, the born-again combat vet had been deferred for work as a Defense Department civilian technocrat.

Russert's campaign press releases began hammering on the inconsistencies. "Even his description of his military record varies from article to article." Finally, the consolidated clippings were passed to some reporters who were scheduled to have lunch with the young GOP challenger.

As the reporters sat down to a luncheon interview, the first thing the candidate referred to was his Vietnam service. The reporters, programmed for action by Russert, reported the candidate's false boasts along with the facts of his real-life record. The candidate pulled out of the race. Moynihan ended up scoring the largest plurality of any New York Senate candidate in history.

In September 1986, Joseph P. Kennedy III took his opponent out of a Massachusetts congressional primary with a similar riposte. During a televised debate, his hard-charging rival asserted that the nonprofit oil-importing company run by young Kennedy was doing business with the terrorist government of Libya. "Let me ask you a straight question: Are you in hock to Muammar Qaddafi?" Kennedy looked at his aggressive opponent and replied with an icy calm that won a lot more points than red-faced anger, "Let me just explain to you something about Libya. Libya offered Sirhan Sirhan asylum after he killed my father, and for you to think for a second that Citizens Energy or Citizens Research Corporation would have anything to do

with any oil coming out of Libya is just totally off base."
As they say in Boston, end of story.

METHOD NO. 2: RIDICULE.

In 1944, Franklin Roosevelt was running for a fourth term
against the extremely aggressive Governor Thomas E.
Dewey of New York, who had made his reputation as a
throw-the-book-at-'em prosecutor. But even in the last
months of his life, FDR knew how to turn the tables. Aban-
doning his above-the-battle stance, to focus on just one of
the charges against him, he sent Dewey flying.

The Republicans were claiming that Roosevelt had
abused his office: that he had, among other things, dispatched a destroyer to retrieve his dog, allegedly left behind on a tour of Alaska. Speaking at a Washington black-
tie dinner given by the Teamsters' Union, the President
rose to make a few truly classic remarks. Instead of showing righteous indignation, he delivered a one-man burlesque of the whole affair.

"Republican leaders have not been content with attacks
on me, or my wife, or on my sons," he said. "No, not content with that, they now include my little dog, Fala." The
chuckles began to rise from the audience.

"Well, of course, I don't resent attacks, and my family
doesn't resent attacks, but Fala does resent them," FDR
continued as the laughter crested. "You know, Fala is
Scotch, and being a Scottie, as soon as he learned that the
Republican fiction writers had concocted a story that I had
left him behind on the Aleutian Islands and had sent a
destroyer back to find him—at a cost to the taxpayers of
two or three or eight or twenty million dollars—his Scotch
soul was furious." His voice heavy with mock mournful-
ness, the President concluded, "He has not been the same
dog since."

By attacking Roosevelt, the Republicans had hoped to

draw him out of the White House into a head-to-head with Dewey. With the President's tongue-in-cheek rejoinder, their strategy withered. As the Democratic National Committee announced in the aftermath of what became quickly known as the "Fala speech," "The race is now between the President's dog and Dewey's goat."

A letter that FDR sent to Congresswoman-elect Helen Gahagan Douglas in the weeks just after the 1944 election gives a vivid portrait both of how Roosevelt viewed the short, brooding Dewey and how satisfied he was with his hardball political tactic:

> Things here settled down immediately into the usual routine, though I am still mad at the little black man and will continue to be so. I think it is good for me. It was the rottenest, dirtiest campaign I have ever taken part in in thirty-four years—but my strategy worked. At the Teamsters dinner on September twenty-fifth, I deliberately wrote out a speech with the objective in mind of making Governor Dewey angry. It worked. He got angrier and angrier and in this part of the country lost thousands of votes by doing so.
>
> Do come East and see us soon.

METHOD NO. 3: JUJITSU.

This technique, where you use the force of the opponent's own attack to bring him down, was named by Jeff Greenfield, an ABC correspondent who was once a speechwriter for Robert Kennedy.

My favorite example is the 1975 reelection campaign of a Virginia state senator, Joseph Gartlan.

Gartlan's opponent that year was making a big issue of busing, nailing Gartlan hard for failing to support a constitutional amendment that would end the busing of school-children to achieve racial integration. The measure, if adopted by enough states, would have written into the U.S. Constitution a specific ban on the busing of school-children from one district to another.

In an area where most children were white and attended public school, the busing issue began to cut. The people of northern Virginia were not at all enthusiastic about having their kids bused off to the mean streets of downtown D.C. Polls showed that the incumbent was getting killed, particularly in the normally Democratic working-class areas. Just a few days from election, it seemed to be all over for him.

Then, the Friday before the election, his consultant Arnold Bennett created a campaign flyer that was a true work of art. It was a simple offset sheet that contained a picture of the Washington Monument with a school bus aimed directly at it. The text hit the Republican opponent right between the eyes: "John Watkins believes it is constitutional to bus your children into Washington."

The literature was staggeringly effective, and, in an odd way, accurate. Watkins had indeed argued the need for a constitutional amendment to prevent interdistrict busing. He had said that without such an amendment the courts could not prevent such busing. He had in fact implied that it might be judged constitutional to "bus your children into Washington."

With this audacious reversal, the incumbent was able to seize a highly explosive charge and redirect the blast to the man who had lit the fuse. By distributing the material only to working-class neighborhoods, where the busing issue was cutting politically, he avoided upsetting his more liberal constituents who drove Volvos and sent their children to private school. By striking just three days before election, he made counterattack impossible.

Sometimes the more direct approach is best.

In 1952, a young East Texan named Jack Brooks was in his first race for the U.S. House of Representatives. Not yet thirty, he too found himself the target of red-baiting. Pepperlike charges were raised against him, but unlike Pepper he had no intention of pretending that the attacks had not occurred. Speaking to a large meeting of voters, he aired the charges and his response. "I fought the fascists for five years in World War Two; I own a shotgun back at home and I'll *shoot* any man who calls me a Communist."

It had a certain Texas ring to it. It also ended the bogus charges. Brooks went on to serve his district in Washington through four decades.

PART III

DEALS

Chapter Eight

Only Talk When It Improves the Silence

"Whaddaya hear?"

For a good part of the 1980s, that was the first thing I'd hear from Tip O'Neill in the morning.

If I called him up at home, it would be "Morning, Chris. Whaddaya hear?" It would be the same if I caught him on the car phone heading to the Capitol to preside over a full-dress debate on Nicaragua or on his way to National Airport to give a fund-raising speech in Cleveland.

He'd switch on the vacuum cleaner whenever I entered his back-room office. "Whaddaya hear? Anything special out there?"

Then would come the silence, the long impatient pause lying heavy in the morning air.

That would be the cue. People who worked for him would sit there, edgy as prizefighters, ready to punch that silence to death. We would throw everything we had at it: every mental clip from the newspapers, that morning and all through the weekend. I would hit the interesting points made on the interview and talk shows, what the national columnists had said. If the President had done anything or I had heard that the White House *might* be intending anything, that too would come rushing out.

Then there was the internal news, the scuttlebutt, the complaints in the cloakroom, the shots taken at "the leadership" at meetings, every possible tidbit about what "the Republicans" were up to. After this short history of the world, what was there to say?

Then more relentless silence. Finally I would feel the pull of one last great inhalation of facts, figures and gossip. "Anything else I ought to know?"

When another aide, whether the general counsel or the rawest intern, entered, the challenge would be thrown up anew: "Anything special, Kirk?" "Whaddaya hear out there, Johnny?"

This was how Tip O'Neill, victor in fifty straight local political ballotings, unchallenged Speaker of the Massachusetts legislature and unchallenged Speaker for ten years of the U.S. House of Representatives, began his day. In a world where information is money in the bank, the tough old Speaker had begun the day-long negotiation for every cent he could get his giant hands on.

Tip O'Neill loves information and dismisses those who lack it. "That guy would ask me how to vote on a quorum call," he said of one hopelessly unaware former member. And while O'Neill respected his staff, even bragged about us, there was one failing he would not suffer: being out of the know. For a leader and his lieutenants not to know what "the members" were up to was the national equivalent of that worst political sin, losing touch with the people back home in the district. For the leadership, the House *is* the district.

To watch Tip O'Neill listening in a meeting or quietly intimidating his staff is to understand silence as an art form. The few syllables emitted from this huge and de-

manding presence would bring a flood tide of words, rushing desperately to fill the void.

Men and women who rise to power in large organizations, whether public or private, political or corporate, succeed through a keen understanding of the institution
and its members, gained not by speaking but by listening,
not by barking commands but by asking the right questions.

During my years of working with all stripes of politicians, the good and the bad, the gentlemen and the ogres,
I've seen the varied uses of silence. A profession which
advertises itself with words often performs its most critical
deeds in crafty silence. Each working morning, Tip
O'Neill would intimidate his staff into playing Gracie
Allen to his George Burns, complete with cigar. "Tell 'em
about your brother, Gracie," Burns would say, and the rest
of the show would be Allen's, with long-suffering George
puffing his accompaniment.

But that is only one version of the silent treatment.
O'Neill has been accused of "listening with his tongue,"
talking and jousting to get people talking themselves. Others use a more soft-spoken approach. Congressman Richard A. Gephardt of Missouri became leader of the
Democratic Caucus in the House of Representatives
largely on his willingness to be an audience for them.
While others did the preaching, the ribbing and the towel-
snapping, Gephardt listened and laughed. He became an
expert on his colleagues, knowing how they thought, what
they cared about, what made them tick. He became the
best head-counter in the House, able to call the yeas and
the nays within three votes of the final result.

"I ain't never learned nothin' talkin,' " Lyndon Johnson
used to say, and this old-breed political motto still guides
even such young-men-in-a-hurry as Dick Gephardt. More
than courtesy is at work. The Missouri Congressman lis-

tens to his colleagues with a power that most politicians cannot command at the top of their lungs.

Silence doesn't just get you hard intelligence; it can make things happen. Real power on Capitol Hill is wielded by men who know that silence can be a sharper tool than rhetoric and that noise is rarely tantamount to action. Don't let the high ceilings and the chandeliers fool you. There are only two businesses conducted on green felt tables: pool-sharking and lawmaking.

It is in this realm of sharp elbows and deceptive quiet that Senator Edmund S. Muskie of Maine established his great reputation as a legislator.

Muskie is famous for his failure as a Presidential candidate in 1972. First there was his stubbornness. He refused to commit himself on how a Muskie Administration would bring an end to the Vietnam War. That permitted George McGovern to move to his left and thereby outflank him on the issue that mattered most to Democratic voters in that election year. Second, he had a table-thumping temper that could boil to the point of tears, as it did that snowy February afternoon in New Hampshire when a right-wing newspaper editor, William Loeb of the *Manchester Union Leader*, ridiculed his wife's demeanor.

Yet the two traits that proved so detrimental to his Presidential ambitions were his best assets as a deal-making senator.

Most senators look forward to committee markup sessions, when the laws are actually written, with resignation. The hours pass slowly. There are lots of numbers and nuts-and-bolts stuff to diddle with, and few if any obvious prizes to be won. The Washington press corps has flashier items to cover than sixteen middle-aged legislators arguing over spending estimates. Muskie was different. He began a markup with the quiet determination of a young boy unpacking his Lionel train layout in preparation for Christmas. He had a sure sense that a little work and a little time would bring a solid, predictable measure of accomplishment.

The record shows that Muskie's penchant for the legislative nitty-gritty, tortoiselike pace and attentiveness to colleagues paid off. The Senator from Maine was personally responsible for the last great round of positive, landmark federal legislation: the Clean Water Act of 1972, which required that every industry end pollution of the country's rivers and lakes; the Budget Control Act of 1974, which gave Congress the means if not the will to control the federal budget; the Clean Air Act of 1977, which challenged the mighty auto industry.

As an assistant to the Senate Budget Committee, I was for two years an eyewitness to the Muskie method of operation. I saw at close range how a pol can get his way not with the violence of the street mugger but with the stealth of a veteran pickpocket.

Here's the M.O. On days when the committee sat, Muskie would arrive a few minutes before ten and take his seat at the head of the table. One at a time, his colleagues arrived. Senatorial pleasantries were exchanged. Photos were taken for the *Washington Post*, the *New York Times* and the wire services.

"Are there any statements?" the chairman would ask.

The other senators would then seize the opportunity to put their thoughts on the record. Statements were read. Cameras whirred. Positions were espoused. This was the part that Muskie's colleagues liked. Handsome Senator Ernest "Fritz" Hollings of South Carolina would shoot a colorful barb at one target or another. His rich baritone would bring titters even before the punch line. Senator Walter "Fritz" Mondale of Minnesota would make a high-toned statement about the importance of "full funding" for a child development program. California's Alan Cranston, his mien severe, would take a shot at CIA spending and reiterate the need for "accountability." Senator Bob Dole would arrive last and needle a vulnerable liberal, Mondale being the usual target. Delaware's Joseph R. Biden, Jr., would repeat without blinking an eye a joke heard in the same committee room and in front of the same audience the day before.

Eventually there was a sea change. The camera tripods were collapsed. Then, just as predictably, the senators began to drift off, to meet constituents, to address a downtown luncheon they had "gotten themselves committed to," or to attend another committee session.

Throughout the markup session, Muskie never left his chair. Hours passed as the work of the committee proceeded. The stomachs of his colleagues would begin to growl, but the chairman would hold to his seat.

"Anyone else want to speak?" he would say, looking with conscious patience from one straggler to the other. Slowly, as the short hand moved past one o'clock, he accumulated a small handful of slips beside his left hand. Those were the proxies of his departed colleagues. Each slip was a little different, expressing the Senator's own priorities, but all of them reflected, one way or another, the chairman's as well. "Anyone else?" he would say, slowly shuffling the tiny folded papers. "Does anyone else have anything to say?" As the room emptied, the chairman's pockets filled with proxies.

The Senator who wins at legislative deal-making is rarely the man with "new ideas." Far more frequently he is the one tough enough to endure the process. Edmund Muskie won not because he was the smartest man in the room—although he may well have been—but because he was willing to be the last man in the room.

Muskie's rule was as dry as leaves: *Only talk when it improves the silence.* Getting legislation passed *his* way, not just the titles, but line by line, was Muskie's obsession. While others postured, he listened, speaking up only when a favorite program was threatened. When his colleagues became restless, he waited. His waiting was legendary: his staff nicknamed him "Iron Pants." For him, it was not the debating points, or the statements of conscience and position, or the media attention, but the bill itself.

Time was Muskie's soul brother. Where his counterpart in the House would draft a budget plan in three days, Muskie's committee would take that many weeks. Each of his great environmental bills took two years, an entire Congress, to be enacted. The Clean Water Act took forty-five days of markups and forty-four sessions of the House-Senate conference.

Once, in a battle over the Clean Air Act, Muskie seemed ready to let the U.S. auto industry shut down. Under an existing statute, the assembly lines would be halted on environmental grounds unless Congress passed remedial legislation. His adversary at the time was Congressman John D. Dingell of Michigan, a legislator known for his avid support of the auto industry. When told that failure to reach agreement with the House would mean a shutdown, Muskie gave a brief but classic response: "There aren't any auto works in Maine."

Muskie's celebrated temper added a barometric factor to his conferences with the House. A conferee's greatest asset is a reputation for being "difficult." Normally, Muskie wore a Mount Rushmore countenance. But when he wished to feel goaded, his temper would erupt and in stages: first, a minor tremor, than a greater burst, then progressing up the Richter scale to a full, shattering explosion. Few people wanted to see it run its course. Three centuries ago, La Rochefoucauld wrote an assessment that fits Muskie precisely. "Fortune sometimes uses our faults for our advancement," he wrote. "Some people are so tiresome that their merits would go unrewarded were it not that we want to get them out of the way."

One morning I was returning with Senator Muskie from a 7 A.M. live interview with CBS. Riding through the morning rush hour up to Capitol Hill, I was made to feel personally responsible for the traffic. I had an overwelming urge to bolt from the car, shrieking at each car ahead, "Hey, please pull over, won't you! You're upsetting SENATOR MUSKIE!"

Imagine spending weeks sitting with that sort of man in a small room in the Capitol caverns. No wonder men were willing to make concessions to him. No wonder they set their sights low coming into those potentially endless meetings and took anything they could get, unreasonably rating each modest sucess a major triumph. Some walked away happy that they had achieved roughly—*very* roughly—what they set out to achieve; others were simply glad they could walk away.

Edmund Sixtus Muskie was a man who judged his success very coldly. On my last day on his staff, I told him that if ours were a parliamentary form of government he would have become Prime Minister. Like Lyndon Johnson and Hubert Humphrey, he was a great legislator. In a system where the legislative leader was also the head of government, the hugely productive Senator from Maine would have eventually taken his place at the top.

Listening patiently, Muskie looked at me and then said in a voice as dry as the rocky crags of Maine, "But we don't, do we?"

Refusing to speculate, Muskie remained fastened to the real world of the U.S. Senate and his own strengths in contending with it. For him, even his volcanic temper was an "element of style." When the crunch came on an issue, he possessed an unlimited vat of righteous indignation. "Why should I compromise?" he would yell. "I don't need a bill *that* bad."

As politicians go, Muskie was a heavyweight, if a flawed one. He became a "senators' senator" because of a maddening degree of concentration and an awesome inner rage that he found a way to make productive.

Alexis de Tocqueville, that great French chronicler of American democracy, observed the power that men such as Muskie have in wielding political influence. "We succeed in enterprises which demand the positive qualities we possess, but we excel at those which also make use of our *defects*."

That is a substantial lesson. In any negotiating situation, the race is rarely to the swift. Congress rarely completes its annual business on schedule, because as in any other deal some key members recognize that they can wait out their opponents. The negotiator who keeps his powder dry usually enjoys a decisive edge.

The "Only talk when it improves the silence" rule played a major part in this century's history.

Two of the great orators of our language were Winston Churchill and the younger, less seasoned John F. Kennedy. Still, in the lives of both these men who used words as a path to deeds, the critical turn of fate came when they held their tongues.

May 9, 1940, was a terrible day in British history. Hitler had just invaded Holland and Belgium. Prime Minister Neville Chamberlain's policy of appeasement lay in ruins. Summoned to the Cabinet Room at eleven o'clock that night, Winston Churchill listened to Chamberlain trying to make his fateful decision on the succession. His shattered government could no longer retain the confidence of Parliament or the British people. Chamberlain was now admitting the inevitable. The choice had come down to Churchill, First Lord of the Admiralty, who had warned for a decade of the need to challenge Hitler, and Lord Halifax, the appeasing Foreign Secretary, a peer and therefore a member of the House of Lords.

The three were now seated in the Cabinet Room. Later that night, Chamberlain would have to present to King George VI—who liked Halifax—his resignation and perhaps his recommendation for a successor.

"Can you see any reason, Winston," the Prime Minister asked, "why in these days a peer should not be Prime Minister?"

> Usually I talk a great deal, but on this occasion I was silent [Churchill wrote later]. As I remained silent, a very long pause ensued. Then, at length, Halifax spoke. He said that his position as a Peer, out of the House of Commons, would make it very difficult for him to discharge the duties of Prime Minister in a war like this. He spoke for some minutes. By the time it was finished, it was clear that the duty would fall upon me—had in fact fallen upon me. On this, the momentous conversation came to an end.

Winston Churchill, whose voice would provide the wartime roar for the British lion, said absolutely nothing. He simply gazed silently out the window, onto the street below. The next day, Britain had its greatest Prime Minister.

John F. Kennedy made similar use of silence a generation later.

In October 1962, the United States received confirmation that the Soviet Union was in the process of deploying intermediate-range nuclear missiles on the island of Cuba. The discovery placed the two great superpowers on what appeared to be the slippery slope to World War III.

During the final, unnerving days of that Cuban Missile Crisis, President John F. Kennedy received two conflicting messages from Nikita Khrushchev, General Secretary of the U.S.S.R. The first was conciliatory. It offered to re-move the I1-28 missiles from the island if the United States would simply promise not to support another inva-sion attempt like the one attempted the year before in the Bay of Pigs. The second cable, received a half day later, was belligerent. It demanded an outright quid pro quo: the Soviets would remove their missiles from Cuba if we, the United States, removed ours from Turkey.

With American planes poised for attack on the Cuban missile sites, JFK considered his final strategy. Acting upon the advice of his brother, Attorney General Robert Kennedy, he decided to ignore the second Khrushchev message, thereby finessing the question of the Turkish bases, and respond to the first cable.

The gambit worked. The next morning word came from the Kremlin that the missiles would be crated and returned to the Soviet Union. The world's first nuclear stand-off was resolved. The man whose words are now engraved in the granite of Arlington National Cemetery performed his greatest service at the moment he and his advisers had the brazen self-control to say nothing at all.

I have seen the same tactic used on the street corner.

In February 1974, a wealthy young congressional can-didate had just returned from his big meeting with Meade Esposito, then the Democratic chief of Brooklyn. "It was dynamite," he said, buoyantly slamming the door behind him. "I can't believe how well it went."

Across the room, the old political operative Paul Corbin sat bare-chested at the telephone. He was staying at the St. Regis, working the phones. Corbin had taught the young Robert Kennedy to be wary of New York politicians, and he was still wary.

"What'd he say, Sam?"

"It was just unbelievable. Esposito was friendly right from the start. He said he'd heard good things about me.

His people say it's good having me in the district. Paul, he was so darn . . . *supportive!"*

The first question mark was beginning to form on the candidate's account. "Sam, what did he say, goddammit? What did he say about an endorsement?"

The neophyte's enthusiasm was faltering. "It wasn't what he said, exactly, but how he said it. You just had to be there. I can't tell you how *positive* it was."

"What'd he say, Sam?"

"He didn't say anything."

"That's right, Sam. He didn't say anything."

In 1974, when I was making my long-shot race for Congress in Pennsylvania, I asked the Congressman from the adjoining district whether he would endorse me. He looked me sincerely in the face and said, "Not publicly."

Now, what he said did not hurt my feelings. On the contrary, I felt that it was just another way of saying, "Well, sure, *privately.*" But "Not publicly" is hardly the sort of ringing endorsement that would move large numbers of voters to my camp. In terms of political currency, it was not something you took to the bank. Still, at the time, the Congressman's noncommittal statement meant a great deal to me. It suggested that he was rooting for me. Those words didn't cost him anything. If I won, he could say he had been plugging for me—I believe he was. If I lost, he could offer solace—"not publicly," of course.

The more you practice, the better you get. Ask a pro for a favor and he'll return the question: "Why didn't you ask me sooner?" The implication is benign. The retort implies not only a certain congeniality but also a mild slap of rebuke. *You* were the one who blew it, not he. One of the biggest mistakes you can make when dealing with a pol is attaching significance to words he does not actually say, to commitments he does not actually make.

Senator Warren Magnuson, the man who spent all those

poker evenings at the Roosevelt White House, had a delightful method for fielding difficult questions from constituents back home. As he wandered through a crowd, people would be calling out to him, "What about the tax bill?" "What about that consumer protection agency?" "How do you stand on gun control?" To each and all he had the same masterly response, "Don't worry about me. I'm all right on *that* one."

Chapter Nine

Always Concede on Principle

> If fascism comes to America, it'll be called anti-fascism.
>
> —HUEY LONG

Swaziland is a small independent kingdom in southern Africa. As a Peace Corps volunteer in that country, I sat in a government office late one morning waiting for our monthly meeting with the Minister of Commerce, Simon Xhumalo. Around the table sat a tense group—government officials, United Nations advisers and a handful of American volunteers, all involved in the country's program to encourage small business.

Morale was low: the Ministry seemed disappointed with the progress being made, and some of us were frustrated by the enormous job, made more difficult by cultural differences and lack of realistic communication from the top. Something was ready to blow.

Finally, the Minister took his place at the head of the conference table, his eyes sharply scanning the assembled English, Americans and Swazis. As usual, his pudgy neck was constricted by a bright white shirt, its collar a full size too tight.

Then he spoke, in words that proved that the politician's craft knows no cultural boundaries. "All the people in this room have one thing in common," he said, the whites of his eyes flashing from one testy face to the next—just enough pause to mature the moment.

"We are all *dissatisfied.*"

He then embarked on a long agenda of frustrations, sprinkled lightly, then more heavily, with the thwarted ambitions his people had for their country.

It was brilliant politics. Rather than deny the anger that filled the room, he had saluted it. Rather than deflect criticism, he joined in the protest. In a situation that seemed to demand he play defense, he rushed blithely to the attack. Yes, *we* are dissatisfied. Yes, *we* are frustrated, because, yes, *all of us* are united in *our* ambitions for this country of his.

That grandly eloquent final point was the kicker. For if we were not frustrated by our inability to get something done for the Swazi people, then we must be moved by concerns about our own interests and convenience—something none of us would or could be willing to acknowledge.

Simon Xhumalo, Minister of Commerce, Industry and Mines of the kingdom of Swaziland, was teaching a vital political lesson to those who had come to show him some tricks of economic development. In a surprising number of circumstances, the best way to achieve the goal is to concede the argument. *Okay,* he was saying, you are all upset with the way things are going around here. Guess what? I agree with you.

Like the drab architecture of their government buildings, the concession on principle was a hand-me-down of late British imperial policy. The maneuver was executed as follows: Faced with unruly Asian or African colonials dead set on independence, the defenders of Empire would delay until the pressure for freedom was irreversible. Then, a few minutes before midnight, Whitehall would offer the colony its independence in exchange for a few concessions. The nationalists would get to have their own flag; the British would retain control of the port and the power plant.

"Yield to a man's tastes," Edward Bulwer-Lytton wrote in 1835, "and he will yield to your *interests*." There has been no slicker practitioner of this old Tory bargaining tactic than Ronald Reagan. There is no better teacher of how to get exactly what you want by telling the other guy exactly what he wants to hear.

His most virtuoso turn of this trick was displayed in selling Congress on the MX missile in the spring of '83. Like a weatherbeaten old skipper, Reagan used the gale force of his opponents' arguments to tack across the wind, selling the MX by making the case against it.

To appreciate the scope of this achievement, imagine for a moment all the bombs dropped by both sides on Europe in World War II. Think of all the newsreel footage beginning with the Blitz: the assault on Normandy and the race through France, the brutal terror of the Eastern front, the carpet-bombing of Germany, the destruction of Cologne and Dresden. Now combine all these mental pictures into one giant explosion, the combined destructive power of all the bombs dropped by the U.S. Army Air Forces, the Royal Air Force and the Luftwaffe in one convulsion.

That's the force of one MX missile.

Yet the weapon is fatally flawed. At 200,000 pounds, it is impossible to hide. By the time it is deployed, Soviet satellites already have each one in their cross hairs.

This dangerous vulnerability gives the MX its use-it-or-lose-it aspect. If fired first, its ten warheads strike ten targets. Undischarged, it becomes a choice target: a ten-strike in the game of nuclear terror. One Soviet silo-buster zaps ten American warheads in one stroke.

What results from the deployment of such a weapon is a Dr. Strangelove mind-set: to be useful, missiles like the MX must be launched and on their way within minutes of first warning or else be smothered in their underground cribs. As they used to say in the old West, this makes for an itchy trigger finger.

The early and decisive critics of the MX were not moralists of the far left, but moderates who believed that the country should be building its strategic capability on a sounder basis. Instead of gigantic, immobile systems like the MX, they argued, the United States should deploy smaller, lighter missiles that could be placed on mobile launchers, thereby evading detection. Rather than inviting a first strike, these "Midgetmen" missiles would make it impractical by miniaturizing, multiplying and moving the targets. A nation armed with a large number of these weapons dispersed secretly throughout its territory could deter attack by threatening retaliation with much of its nuclear firepower still intact.

In the face of these arguments, President Reagan launched a major campaign for the MX. Congressmen and senators were brought to the White House for hi-tech briefings. The President made a prime-time TV address to pitch the product, using state-of-the-art video graphics. He told the people sitting in their living rooms that they should not worry about the MX's appalling vulnerability. His experts had solved that problem. To avoid being cornered into "using or losing," he would place all one hundred MX missiles so close together that an attack on one would create such an explosion that it would destroy any other Soviet missile entering the area. He called it "dense pack."

The speech was a clinker. People began referring to "dunce pack." All the Soviets would have to do, some critics said, was to equip their missiles with a timer: the warheads would converge over the MXs and detonate simultaneously. In an effort to make the MX less of a sitting duck, he was simply offering the enemy a flock of sitting ducks in one nest.

Reagan critics, such as Representative Edward J. Markey of Massachusetts, were delighted. "In every beauty parlor and barbershop in the country people were saying to themselves, 'I finally understand this dense-pack thing and it's the stupidest idea I ever heard of!' "

Congress agreed. Meeting in a lame-duck session called by the President, the House voted to postpone the MX issue until the following spring. The lame ducks had disposed of the sitting ducks!

But the President was not ready to give up. Having failed to sell the MX on its merits, he reversed field. Rather than fight his critics, he joined them—rhetorically, that is.

Yes, the arms race needed to end. Rather than stockpiling more nuclear weapons, the United States and the Soviet Union should be reducing the number of their missiles. In fact, we should work toward eliminating such weapons entirely.

Yes, his critics were right about the matter of vulnerability. The big multiheaded missiles like the MX should be replaced by small, single-headed missiles that could be concealed on mobile launchers.

This second concession was showcased in a report by the President's Commission on Strategic Forces, chaired by General Brent Scowcroft, which acknowledged the need to deemphasize the multiwarheaded missile. It said that Midgetmen, which could survive a first strike, were the wave of the future. In fact—now hear this!—deployment of the MX was an essential catalyst of the transition. To get Midgetmen, we needed to deploy MX as an "interim" approach, a bargaining chip in moving the Soviets toward more "survivable" weapons.

And with this, Reagan carried the day. Congressional moderates were so thrilled with their success in "educating" the President on their new-breed Midgetman doctrine that they buckled to his demand for the MX.

Such congressmen as Wisconsin's Les Aspin and Tennessee's Albert Gore, Jr., proud of their arms-policy sophistication, fell hook, line and sinker for the Presidential ploy. In exchange for a philosophical concession applying to the future, they bought the President's position on the only tangible issue on the table. Within a few months it became clear, however, that the Administration had no intention of pursuing the reformers' approach. When the arms reduction talks began, the President's negotiating team let it be known that the single-warhead, mobile missile would be the first item up for elimination.

The result was embarrassing. In voting to deploy the MX, key members of Congress adopted a *policy* of eliminating big, land-based, multiheaded missiles and a *program* of deploying them. Fifty "bargaining chips," each carrying the explosive power of two hundred Hiroshimas, now crouch ready for action under the windswept plains of Wyoming.

The popular view is that Ronald Reagan was a last-minute compromiser who waited until the eleventh hour of a negotiation before grudgingly agreeing to the other side's demands. Actually, the compromise was far less than meets the eye: a surrender not on the substance but on the principle at stake, giving the impression of compromise by telling his adversaries what they want to hear. Oftentimes, he was simply recasting his final argument in his opponents' words.

By conceding the main theories at issue, Ronald Reagan turned a defeat in late 1982 to a spring victory in 1983. By packaging his objective in the language and premise favored by the opposition, he carried the day.

Another case in point was Reagan's lobbying for military aid to the rebels fighting the Communist government of Nicaragua.

The press has often looked upon Reagan's championing of the tax cut in 1981 as one of his greatest triumphs. Common sense should have told them that cutting taxes is about as hard as handing out free beers at a midsummer baseball game. Getting Congress to fight some murky civil war in Central America is another matter. Here the President was dealing not with Americans looking for a break on April 15, but with a public increasingly wary of "another Vietnam," and a guerrilla force seen as both brutal and ineffective, its cause fatally entangled with the forces of the earlier Somoza dictatorship. The fact that Reagan succeeded even temporarily is testament to his clever negotiating tactics.

As in the case of MX, the Administration first tried the hard sell. In the spring of 1986, White House communications director Patrick Buchanan let loose a fusillade at those Democrats opposing the President on Nicaragua. In an article appearing in the *Washington Post*, he branded them as "co-guarantors of the Brezhnev Doctrine in North America"—in other words, of voting the Moscow line, taking their signals from the enemy.

The article was a blunder. Rather than forge a consensus, it helped to polarize the debate. House Democrats stood their ground and voted down the Reagan Nicaragua policy. Many who did cited Buchanan's vitriolic attack. The campaign for military aid seemed headed for defeat.

In June, the President reconnoitered and, just as in the MX case, shifted tactics. He ceased arguing for military aid to the "contras" and started to sound like a critic of the policy. In a televised address, given on the eve of a key congressional vote, he once again *conceded on principle*:

Yes, the United States has had a sorry history in the region. "I ask first for help in remembering our history in Central America so we can learn from the mistakes of the past. Too often in the past, the United States failed to identify with the aspirations of the people of Central America for freedom and a better life."

Yes, there has been brutality by the rebels. "I know that members of Congress and many Americans are deeply troubled by allegations of abuse by leaders of the armed resistance. I share your concerns. Even though some of these charges are Sandinista [government] propaganda, I believe such abuses have occurred in the past and are intolerable."

Yes, we must end the Somoza connection. "As President, I will insist on civilian control of all military forces, that no human-rights abuses be tolerated; that any form of corruption be rooted out; that American aid go only to those committed to democratic principles. The United States must not permit this democratic revolution to be betrayed nor allow a return to the hated repression of the Somoza dictatorship."

Yes, my critics are patriotic. "I know that even the Administration's harshest critics in Congress hold no brief for Sandinista representations. I know that no one in Congress wants to see Nicaragua become a Soviet military base."

The whole tone and construction of the address made it clear that there were Americans of goodwill on both sides of the Nicaragua issue. Many of those listening to the speech felt that in terms of language and sensibility, it could have been drafted by a Democrat.

The fact is, it was—specifically, by Bernard Aronson, a former speechwriter for Walter Mondale and Jimmy Carter. Quite literally, the President and his men, Buchanan included, had judiciously chosen to win their goal even if that meant making their opponents' arguments. The maneuver worked. Thirty members of congress shifted position and voted to release the money to the rebels.

By conceding the principle at issue, Reagan manipulated his critics into accepting his policy.

Smart move.

The conventional view is that politicians like to argue and that they like to win arguments. Actually, they often have other priorities. The smart ones focus less on the principle than on the objective, the tangible result at issue. When sitting down to deal, they always separate the principle at stake from the actual stakes. Then, with the air thick with melodrama, they concede on the principle— and rake in the chips.

As Machiavelli advised, a great leader must be both lion and fox. In cutting taxes, Reagan loved to play the lion. In prosecuting an immensely unpopular war all those years, he showed he could also play the fox.

PART IV

REPUTATIONS

Chapter Ten

Hang a Lantern on Your Problem

> Jimmy Carter. Jimmy Carter? How can that be?
> I don't even know Jimmy Carter, and as far as
> I know, none of my friends know him, either.
> —W. AVERELL HARRIMAN

Nineteen seventy-four—Jimmy Carter's last year as governor of Georgia. Sharing a beer one night in the Governor's Mansion with his media adviser, Gerald Rafshoon, Carter was in a serious mood. He moved from the personal business they had been discussing to the big picture.

"We've got to really start thinking about the themes for this Presidential thing. I think I've got them pretty well worked out," Rafshoon recalls him saying. Then on a long yellow legal pad Carter wrote down what he saw as his assets:

> not a lawyer
> Southerner
> farmer
> 300 days a year to campaign (would be out of office)
> ethics
> not part of Washington scene
> religious

That night and in the many months that followed, Rafshoon and the others in the small Carter cadre joked that most people would consider the points on that legal pad to be downright liabilities. "But I think we can make them into assets," the governor had said that night, and he went on to prove it.

Rather than hide those aspects of his background that would conventionally make him ineligible to run for President, Carter brandished them. In the two-year campaign that would take him to the White House, he perfected his litany: "I'm not a lawyer, even though I have great respect for them, and my son is a lawyer. I've never worked in Washington. I'm not a senator or a congressman. I've never met a Democratic President."

He would even tease audiences with his reverse-chic credentials as a political dark horse, by describing a recent poll that asked people about the various big-name Democrats currently "being mentioned" as possible Presidential candidates. Carter would then recite the roll of honor in complete deadpan: Senator Hubert Humphrey, Senator Henry Jackson, Senator Birch Bayh of Indiana, Governor Hugh L. Carey of New York; Governor Jerry Brown of California.

"There's even a Georgian on the list, who scored a one percent in the poll," he would add with a smile. Pregnant pause. "His name is . . . Julian Bond."

Carter knew the conventional view of what a Presidential candidate ought to be: a lawyer, a senator or governor, someone with foreign-policy experience. He also recognized that public attitudes are more flexible. People would accept a candidate with a vastly different claim on the office. The important thing was for the candidate himself to explain his somewhat offbeat resumé.

Carter's successor, Ronald Reagan, trusted the same political principle: it's *always* better to be the bearer of your own bad news.

When Reagan met Walter Mondale in the first Presidential debate of 1984, Reagan's performance raised questions about his abilities. Most baffling was his contention that Social Security was somehow not part of the federal deficit.

But it was not a failure to grasp a particular fact in that first encounter that got people talking; it was his overall performance. *Newsweek,* for example, said he appeared "shaky," that the seventy-three-year-old President might finally be showing his age. In the days immediately afterward, the Monday-morning quarterbacks picked at Reagan with a vengeance. Even some presumed loyalists were critical. Howard H. Baker, Jr., the Republican leader of the Senate, told reporters, "What you saw in the debate was what you see in the Cabinet meetings and leadership sessions." And it got worse. "If the point of this is to get an inside view, you got more of that tonight than I've ever seen in public with Ronald Reagan."

Once the Republicans broke ranks, the recharged opposition could afford to show some unaccustomed restraint. Speaker Tip O'Neill just sprinkled a little pepper. "People in the White House tend to get old mighty quickly," he said at his morning-after press conference. Another Democrat, lacking the subtle touch, said that the President had "drooled" during the debate.

The public furor over Reagan's apparent loss of clarity peaked a few days later with a front-page story in the *Wall Street Journal.* "Is the Oldest U.S. President Now Showing His Age?" "Reagan's Debate Performance Invites Open Speculation on His Ability to Serve."

Democrats smelled blood. For the first time since the campaign began, there seemed to be a possibility of Walter Mondale's upsetting the popular incumbent. If Reagan tripped in their second confrontation, a groundswell could emerge for a more nimble national leader.

Reagan's own corner men were plainly worried. James Baker, White House chief of staff, released the President's most recent medical report, attesting to the fact that he was still "mentally alert." One of his key strategists, Lee Atwater, mapped a contingency plan, to be executed if the President did as poorly in the second debate as he had done in the first: a countrywide firestorm of attacks on Mondale's support of big social programs and opposition to new weapons systems.

The Atwater memo also called for Reagan's people to dismiss the debates as a "bizarre ritual" which had no place in a civilized choosing of Presidents. The feared Reagan fiasco was to be smothered by a "fog machine." The memo continued: "If it's clear that the President did badly, then it's our job to obscure the result. The single most important mission of the fog machine will be to shift the emphasis to Mondale, and to drive up his negative rating."

Meanwhile, the stage was set for the second debate. There would be only one issue: age. There would be only one focus: whether Ronald Reagan showed any signs of his earlier "rambling."

Henry Trewitt, a *Baltimore Sun* correspondent sitting on the debate panel, got right to the point. Citing the Cuban Missile Crisis of 1962, he reminded viewers that no President knows when he might have to face an endurance test of prolonged stress, one that would demand high energy and quick judgment. Did Reagan feel he "would be able to function in such circumstances?"

Reagan was ready. In a tone of mock seriousness he replied, "I will not make my age an issue in this campaign. I am not going to exploit, for political purposes, my opponent's youth and inexperience."

The election was over. Even Mondale had to chuckle— even though he knew that his campaign's one brief, shining moment of opportunity was dissolving in the laughter and applause he heard all around him.

Reagan's comeback had produced an irresistible ten-second "sound bite" for local and network news broadcasts, one that would be repeated and repeated in the days that followed. His own pollsters recorded a positive response from viewers that "went off the charts." In one sentence, the old showman from Hollywood had killed the only issue that might have kept him from a second term.

In slaying the age issue, Reagan had also demonstrated an important lesson of politics: If a question has been raised publicly about your personal background, you need to address the issue personally.

"Hang a lantern on your problem" applies with equal force to cases where you're selling yourself one-to-one and when you're targeting a broader audience. Retail or wholesale, the one durable truth obtains: when in doubt, get it out. If you've done something your boss is not going to like, it is far better that you yourself bring him the bad news. It gives him a perfect opportunity to let his steam off. It shows that you are not trying to put one past him. Most important, it protects him from being surprised and embarrassed by hearing it from someone outside.

Bad news has a habit of spreading. It is always better to create your own trial scene than to let someone else rig one up.

In 1960 the Democratic candidate for President faced persistent questions about his Roman Catholicism. Many people believed there would be an inevitable conflict between JFK's loyalty to the nation and his fidelity to his church. Never before had the voters of this predominantly Protestant country ever allowed a Catholic to gain the Presidency. It was heatedly argued that on matters from education to foreign policy John F. Kennedy would be taking his marching orders from the Vatican.

Kennedy set out to disarm his opponents with his handicap. He went to a well-publicized meeting of a group of Protestant ministers in Houston. The staging of the event was important: traveling to Texas in the first week of the fall campaign, casting himself as the defendant in the case, submitting to be judged by the people who were considered his most skeptical jury.

To underline the David-and-Goliath aspects, Kennedy's

people made two decisions. First, the candidate would go to Houston alone. Second—as Robert Strauss, who was advancing the event, remembers being ordered to do by Lyndon Johnson—put the "meanest, nastiest-looking" of the Texas preachers right up in the first row. The national television audience would have no trouble choosing whom to root for.

Kennedy's message came across clear and appealing. He described America as a country "where no Catholic prelate would tell the President—should he be a Catholic—how to act and no Protestant minister would tell his parishioners for whom to vote." This is a country, he said, "where religious liberty is so indivisible that an act against one church is treated as an act against all."

He concluded by saying that he would resign the Presidency if he ever felt that his conscience conflicted with the national interest. That outlandish promise served a critical purpose. It gave a brilliant line of intellectual retreat to those whose concern about a Catholic President rested not on any visceral bigotry but on the easily imaginable tensions—divorce, birth control, capital punishment—between secular office and religious discipline.

By appearing before the Houston ministers and answering all reasonable questions, he had left his opponents with only the unreasonable ones, such as, Does the United States really want a Catholic President? Anyone who opposed him on religious grounds now was simply a bigot. Sam Rayburn, a doubter before the Houston gambit, felt that Kennedy, the lone gladiator who had walked into the lions' den, had not only avoided being eaten himself, he had triumphed. "As we say in my part of Texas, he ate 'em blood raw."

Kennedy had brilliantly "hung a lantern on his problem." He had established the terms under which he would be judged, had set his own trial date, and had assembled the jury. In an odd way, his own wonderful bit of daring made the judgment at Houston a peremptory acquittal.

The Kennedy family would soon put the rule to another use. When Edward Moore Kennedy, the President's youngest brother, ran for the Senate in 1962, he was attacked by his opponent in a televised debate as a man who "never worked a day in his life," a shot that went to the heart of his candidacy. "If your name were Edward Moore, you would not even be a candidate," his opponent said just as the debate went off the air. Kennedy had had a silver spoon forced down his throat.

The next morning, fate—or strategy—intervened. Kennedy would spend the rest of the campaign telling the story of the hard-working fellow who approached him as he was making the rounds of factory gates and asked, "Hey, Kennedy, are you the one they said last night never worked a day in his life?"

On being assured that he was correct, the veteran dockworker had something to say to the bright-faced young candidate: "Well, let me tell you something, young man, you haven't missed a thing."

This story was identical to one that Kennedy people circulated when JFK was running in the West Virginia primary two years earlier and that always drew a chuckle and knowing looks of agreement from working-class audiences. The little tale drew attention away from the candidate's qualifications—which were thin at the time—to the far less vulnerable matter of wealth. Why should anyone be blamed for being rich? Wouldn't everyone like to be? By facing up to the question, Kennedy had claimed the right to frame it his way. He had pulled the silver spoon from his mouth and held it up for appreciation.

The same ploy was pulled a generation later by another name-brand American.

John D. "Jay" Rockefeller, heir to a far greater fortune

than the Kennedys', faced a more advanced case of the poor-little-rich-kid problem. Not only was he loaded, he had also demonstrated a proclivity for hitting the family treasury for every dime it took to get elected. His quadrennial splurges in nearby West Virginia had become a scandal among Washington reporters.

In 1985 Rockefeller arrived in Washington fresh from a closely contested Senate race. Every journalist in the capital press corps knew exactly how he had won. His television commercials had been running steadily the previous autumn on Washington television stations, simply to pick up the small panhandle of West Virginia that was in the D.C. media area. To win the small town of Harper's Ferry, he was willing to spend hundreds of thousands of dollars in an expensive media market. Washingtonians could only imagine what he had spent to capture the larger television audiences in his adopted state. Here was a man who had already been elected secretary of state and governor twice and still needed millions to win a Senate seat by a squeaker.

So when the elegant young Senator arrived before the annual black-tie dinner of the Washington Press Foundation, he was not exactly the hometown favorite. The average print reporter in the ballroom was lucky to be making $40,000 a year—and hoping to end his career making $60,000. Yet on that evening Jay Rockefeller, squire of Charleston and Georgetown, managed to squash much of the antipathy. In fact, he left them *liking* him.

Rising to make his remarks, he dropped an ice-breaker that will probably be remembered for as long as he stays in Washington: "To those of you who had to fork over seventy-five bucks for your tickets, don't feel so bad. It cost me twelve million to get here tonight."

Rockefeller proved the old rule. The press corps simply wanted the swell standing up before them to admit that he hadn't gotten the job through hard work or any gift of intellect. He didn't claim to be any better than they were. That said, he was accepted into the club. Such performances have a way of defining careers in Washington.

Another West Virginian showed a tougher use of the tactic in 1958. As a U.S. congressman who had always supported the United Mine Workers, Robert C. Byrd felt he had a right to the union's endorsement when he decided to run for the Senate. To his alarm, he received word that a representative of the mighty UMW president, John. L. Lewis, wanted to see him. It was clear to him that the news would be bad, and it was. Meeting the deputy at a hotel, he got it hard across the chin. Lewis and his powerful organization were going to support former Governor William Marlin for the Senate seat. They would support Byrd for reelection to the House.

Byrd listened and the next day held a press conference to make his announcements. First, that he would be a candidate for the United States Senate. Second, that William Marlin would also be a candidate. Third, that John L. Lewis was going to endorse Marlin.

The effect was memorable. Had he remained silent on Lewis' impending endorsement, he would have been trumped by it. His own announcement would have been vastly overshadowed by Marlin's declaration. By making the announcement *for* Marlin and Lewis, he stole his opponents' thunder. Marlin decided to skip that particular race. John L. Lewis ended up endorsing Byrd.

The "Hang a lantern on your problem" rule doesn't work only in the world of elective politics. When applying for any high-powered job, you might want to consider the extraordinary successes of another somewhat less prominent Washingtonian.

In the 1970s, Douglas Bennet served as top aide to Senator Thomas F. Eagleton of Missouri and later to Connect-

icut Senator Abraham A. Ribicoff. Bennet had the ability
to showcase his liabilities so magnificently that they back-
lit his assets, which he rightly believed to be far more
germane.

When the Senate Budget Committee was created in
1974, Bennet applied for the position of staff director. In
his letter of application to the chairman, Edmund S. Muskie of Maine, he brazenly admitted that he lacked a degree
in economics and possessed no experience whatever in
budgeting. He went on to explain that the central challenge facing the new committee, and particularly its chairman, was to convince other senators to accept the
committee's somewhat unpopular mandate to eliminate
unnecessary spending. The committee could no doubt hire
plenty of economists and number-crunchers from the Office of Management and Budget. What the Muskie panel
needed most, however, was a chief of staff with a clear
idea of how to enlist and cultivate a constituency within
the Senate. The committee needed a man who knew senators and their concerns firsthand, someone who had been
a top personal aide, for example.

Bennet got the job and performed masterfully.

Several years later, after a period of uncertain fiscal management, National Public Radio announced it had hired a
new president. The *Washington Post* ran an interview
with the man selected. Douglas Bennet explained the
probable reasons for his appointment.

He admitted that he had no background in either broadcasting or journalism. He said he knew that NPR already
had plenty of people with broadcast experience and a
number of top-flight journalists. The president of National
Public Radio needed to be someone experienced in budget matters and someone who could work with Congress
in obtaining adequate funding.

The applications of "Hang a lantern on your problem"

are abundant. Someone with an obvious physical handicap can put you at ease with a matter-of-fact or even light-hearted reference to it. The mere mention of the problem deflates its relevance, removing it as an unspoken barrier.

In 1986, Barbara A. Mikulski became the first Democratic woman elected to the Senate in her own right, not as someone's widow or daughter. The feisty former city councilwoman from Baltimore won despite questions her opponent raised about her senatorial "stature." The reference was not only to her political pedigree but to her size. Mikulski is four feet, eleven inches tall.

Her standard prop at campaign stump appearances was a small ripple-sided aluminum suitcase. She used it as a platform. When someone introduced her to an audience by offering little more than her name, she was quick as a pistol: "That introduction was as short as I am."

Anyone who has ever worked in public relations will certify that it is better to take the initiative in acknowledging problems, whether they involve your client or a product. The makers of Tylenol discovered the wisdom of this argument after being victimized by bottle-tampering. They gained public sympathy and respect by dealing with the problem openly; stock values were hardly affected. Management gained tremendous goodwill for their product by being open with the consumer even when it hurt. When in doubt, put it out.

"It goes against human nature," Jimmy Carter's press secretary Jody Powell wrote after his White House years, "to stand up of your own free will and volunteer information that is bound to cause nothing but trouble." But as Powell learned in the Iranian hostage-taking and other crises, it is also the only proven means of minimizing the situation. "No matter how smelly it seems to be at first, it always gets worse as it ages."

This is one rule which Ronald Reagan failed to learn

from his predecessors. When his own Iranian arms scandal broke in late 1985, with the disclosure that his agents had been selling arms to the Ayatollah Ruhollah Khomeini, Reagan attempted a cover-up; then he blamed it on his national-security staff; then on his chief of staff, Donald T. Regan. Finally, four months later and twenty points lower in the polls, he admitted to a mistake.

This is one case where he should have learned from history. John F. Kennedy never stood higher in the nation's opinion polls than in the days and weeks after he took sole responsibility for the Bay of Pigs. Where Reagan's refusal to step forward caused months of bad press and congressional investigations, Kennedy's decision to cut his losses made him more popular than ever. "By taking full blame upon himself," writes his aide Ted Sorensen, "he was winning the admiration of both career servants and the public, avoiding partisan investigations and attacks, and discouraging further attempts by those involved to leak their versions and accusations."

By waffling on who was responsible for selling arms to Iran, Ronald Reagan created his own Chinese water torture. Drip by drip, the story leaked out. Point by point, the President's credibility dropped. To get a reading on his slow, humiliating retreat to honesty, compare the following public statements, both of which Reagan made on prime-time national television.

November 13, 1986: "The charge has been made that the United States has shipped weapons to Iran as ransom payment for the release of American hostages in Lebanon, that the United States undercut its allies and secretly violated American policy against trafficking with terrorists. Those charges are totally false."

March 4, 1987: "A few months ago I told the American people that I did not trade arms for hostages. My heart and my best intentions still tell me that's true, but the facts and the evidence tell me it is not. Now, what should happen when you make a mistake is this: you take your knocks, you learn your lessons, and then you move on."

Five months late, the President got it right. Interestingly, his second speech was written by Landon Parvin. Six years earlier this same speechwriter had helped Nancy Reagan solve a serious PR problem.

During her first year in the White House, Mrs. Reagan had been portrayed by the press as a Marie Antoinette figure, someone more concerned with designer clothes than with the condition of her country.

Mrs. Reagan cracked through that image in one glorious night when she appeared before a white-tie dinner of Washington's most powerful journalists and sang, with self-parodying lyrics provided by Landon Parvin, her own show-stopping version of "Secondhand Rose." The woman who had been lambasted for complaining about the state of White House china, the lady with the taste for designer clothing, proved that she was not the aloof Queen of Beverly Hills she'd been depicted.

For the rest of the Reagan Presidency, her popularity continued to rise even as her husband's peaked.

Like the late Robert F. Kennedy who used to disarm campaign audiences by referring to himself as "ruthless," Nancy Reagan had learned to hang a lantern on her problem.

Chapter Eleven

Spin!

You're going to have lunch with the President. The menu is humble pie. You're going to eat every last motherfucking spoonful of it. You're going to be the most contrite sonofabitch this world has ever seen.
—JAMES A. BAKER III

Talk to any Wall Street analyst and you will hear plenty of stories about how much time, effort and creativity companies spend managing expectations and the reaction to their performance. When their stock moves up, it's good news; when it drops, it's "profit-taking"—good news again!

Politicians call that *spin.*

In 1984, Walter Mondale was the early front-runner for the Democratic nomination. His people had pursued a cautious campaign, keyed to winning powerful endorsements and making his nomination seem inevitable. Even in the Iowa caucuses, the first real test of strength, Mondale led with 49 percent to 16 percent for Colorado Senator Gary Hart.

But the strategy fell apart in New Hampshire, where Hart, the young, outdoorsy, "new breed" candidate, won a smashing upset. A week later, Hart upset Mondale again, in the Maine caucuses.

It was now two days before Super Tuesday, the big Democratic primary day of 1984, the day Mondale's plan had called for having the nomination wrapped up. But Hart was now eating him for breakfast, on his way to overwhelming wins in Massachusetts and Florida. Even Dade County was about to vote against Hubert Humphrey's Minnesota protégé. Mondale would be lucky if he could survive the big March primary day with a win in Alabama and Georgia.

Robert Beckel, Mondale's campaign manager, knew that defeat in Georgia would be disastrous. There could be no explaining away Jimmy Carter's Vice President losing Jimmy Carter's home state.

Beckel applied spin, a sophisticated, media-wise extension of "Hang a lantern on your problem." First, you admit you have a crisis. Second, while the public is buying your act, you quickly exploit the situation to turn the heat onto your opponent.

Here's the spin that Beckel put on Super Tuesday: If a defeat in Georgia spelled defeat nationally, victory in Georgia could be read as victory nationally. If Mondale took Georgia, then he was on his way to the White House.

For the thirty-six hours before the primary, Beckel talked to every reporter who would listen. The message: Mondale needed to win in Georgia to keep his campaign alive. If he lost, he was dead; but if he won, he would survive and Hart would have failed.

Beckel had a second plan for primary night. Maybe Mondale was fizzling on the road. Maybe he lacked support in the states that were holding that day's primaries. The networks would still want pictures on primary night. NBC in particular had planned a special hour-long program for 10 P.M. Eastern Standard Time on the early results of Super Tuesday.

Beckel wanted to be sure that the pictures looked damned good for Mondale. His candidate might not pull out the voters in the big primary states, but Beckel could still create a crowd for the cameras in the nation's capital. He put out a call to every known Mondale supporter in

Greater Washington to make sure they were at the Capitol Hilton on primary night. "You've been with Fritz," he told them. "This is one night he needs you. Be there. The whole campaign depends on it."

A respectable "Mondale crowd" gathered. Every paid campaign worker, every Washington lawyer looking for an appointment, every Democratic regular anyone could dig up assembled before the network cameras in the ballroom.

The Mondale rearguard then followed with a tactic that Jerry Bruno had made famous advancing Jack Kennedy in 1960. Partitions were used to make the room as small as possible. "We just *packed* the joint," Beckel said later. "We threw up a partition that made the room a third the size of the ballroom. You couldn't move in the fuckin' place."

The video stage was set for what may have been the greatest election-night postmortem con job in history. Mondale lost seven contests out of nine. But that was just the arithmetic. At a few minutes past ten, campaign director Robert Beckel walked into what looked like a crowded ballroom to tell the faithful that Mondale had just carried Georgia. To the NBC viewing audience, the event played like a victory statement.

Beckel's spin had succeeded famously. When he arrived for a live *Today* show interview the morning after Super Tuesday, Beckel was enthusiastically congratulated by Bryant Gumbel. "Yup," his elated guest beamed, "it's the comeback of the year."

Beckel had accomplished this miracle of news management in two stages: he built his media credibility by openly admitting the problem, and he built on this immediate authenticity by defining the events in the most self-serving way possible. By telling the press that a defeat in Georgia would spell Mondale's doom, he was able to claim a victory on Super Tuesday by the mere force of his candidate's victory in a single, previously overlooked primary state.

Spin was established here and in so many other contexts by progressing one step beyond last chapter's rule. Once established as an honest player by hanging a lantern on your problem, you can exploit that credibility.

Spin is not new to politics. Years earlier a driven young politician had used it to pull an even more dramatic comeback.

On September 22, 1952, a thirty-nine-year-old senator was on a United Airlines flight from Portland to Los Angeles. The next night he would have to give the speech of his career. On a sheaf of souvenir postcards he had pulled from the seatback in front of him, he began to sketch his notes:

"Checkers . . . Pat's cloth coat . . ."

The young man was getting ready to defend his fast-rising political career against charges of corruption. Just as a smart politician can seize control of a situation simply by admitting he or she has a problem, the sophisticated practitioner learns to turn the admission to his quick advantage strategically, spinning the story in a totally new direction.

If anyone needed spin, it was Richard Nixon. He had been elected to the House six years earlier by attacking his opponent's associations with the American left. He had exposed the Communist ties of Alger Hiss and then re-energized his red-baiting to take a Senate seat in 1950. Two years later, he was the Republican nominee for Vice President, running mate to the great World War II hero Dwight D. Eisenhower. Now Nixon was in the middle of a political firestorm. Four days earlier, the *New York Post*, at that time a liberal newspaper, had carried a two-line banner: "Secret Rich Man's Trust Fund Keeps Nixon in Style Far Beyond His Salary."

At first the young Californian flailed helplessly. When

his campaign train was attacked by hecklers, he desperately tried to attribute the fund scandal to his earlier success in cracking the Hiss case. "Ever since I have done that work, the Communists and left-wingers have been fighting me with every possible smear."

It was understandable that Nixon would lose his cool. First of all, the fund in question was not generically all that different from those kept by many other politicians. Moreover, not a penny had gone toward his personal use. But none of these points seemed to matter at the time. The man who had built a career fishing in troubled waters was now foundering in a political typhoon.

In the ensuing days, Nixon was increasingly pressured to leave the ticket. On Saturday, September 20, the *New York Herald Tribune,* the voice of the Republican Party's establishment, was blunt: "The proper course for Senator Nixon in the circumstances is to make a formal offer of withdrawal from the ticket."

Nixon could see the handwriting on the wall: Eisenhower wanted him dumped. That same day, the Eisenhower team called on Senator William F. Knowland, a Californian and an anti-Communist, to join the campaign train. Nixon's substitute was being wheeled into place in broad daylight. When the press asked Eisenhower whether Nixon would remain on the ticket, he told them that his running mate had to be "as clean as a hound's tooth."

On Sunday, more bad news. Harold Stassen, then a figure to be reckoned with in national Republican circles, sent Nixon a telegram urging that he offer his resignation.

Governor Thomas E. Dewey, the key man behind the Eisenhower candidacy, called Nixon with a proposition. The Vice-Presidential nominee should plead his case before the American people, in a nationwide television broadcast. It would not be good enough if the reaction to the program was 60 percent for Nixon and 40 percent against. "If it is ninety to ten," Dewey said, "stay on." Nixon could see that he was being set up to take the fall. Later, Eisenhower himself called. "Tell them everything there is to tell, everything you can remember since the day you entered public life. Tell them about any money you have ever received," Ike insisted.

"General," Nixon asked, "do you think that after the television program an announcement could then be made one way or the other?"

"Maybe," Eisenhower replied.

Nixon went through the roof. "There comes a time in matters like this when you've got to either shit or get off the pot."

Ike, not used to such language from a junior officer, was noncommittal. "Keep your chin up," he said.

Nixon spent the day on the speech. With the broadcast just four hours away, he was about to leave his hotel. He had been discussing with Murray Chotiner, his longtime campaign manager, and William P. Rogers, his future Secretary of State, how the viewing audience should be urged to register their verdict on his public defense. The phone rang. The caller was a "Mr. Chapman," the code name for Governor Dewey. Reluctantly, Nixon took the call.

Dewey: "There has been a meeting of all of Eisenhower's top advisers. They've asked me to tell you that in their opinion at the conclusion of the broadcast you should submit your resignation to Eisenhower."

Nixon: No answer.

Dewey: "Hello? Can you hear me?"

Nixon: "What does Eisenhower want me to do?"

Dewey: "What shall I tell them you are going to do?"

Nixon: "Just tell them that I haven't the slightest idea what I'm going to do, and if they want to find out they'd better listen to the broadcast! And tell them I know something about politics, too."

That night, before the largest TV audience in history—

it was estimated at 58 million—Richard Nixon surprised his enemies.

"My fellow Americans," he began, standing in front of a desk, "I come before you tonight as a candidate for the Vice Presidency and as a man whose honesty and integrity has been questioned."

He then gave his huge, fascinated audience "a complete financial history." Taking the audience back to his youth, Nixon listed all his assets:

> A 1950 Oldsmobile.
> A $3,000 equity in his California home, where his parents were living.
> A $20,000 equity in his Washington house.
> No stocks, no bonds, nothing else.

In his melodramatic appeal, Nixon rhetorically undressed himself. In an age when American families were still extremely private about their financial matters, he was telling the American people exactly what he was *worth*, down to the last penny. At a time when having a mortgage was still viewed as somewhat embarrassing, he was listing his debts on TV! Historian William Manchester chronicled the Checkers episode: "Here, clearly, was a man who knew what it was to worry about getting the kids' teeth straightened, or replacing the furnace, or making the next payment on the very [television] set now tuned to him."

Nixon was also setting up the spin. He was admitting that he needed outside help, that he could not finance a political career on his own resources. It was fine that the Democratic nominee, Governor Adlai E. Stevenson of Illinois, "who inherited a fortune from his father," could run for national office. But in a democracy "a man of modest means" should also be able to make the race. By confessing his slight resources, he was shifting attention from the question of propriety to that of class. "It isn't much," Nixon said after reviewing his entire financial situation, "but Pat and I have the satisfaction that every dime that we've got is honestly ours. I should say this—that Pat doesn't have a mink coat. But she does have a respectable Republican cloth coat."

Nixon was revving. He described how someone had sent his daughters a cocker spaniel and how Tricia had named it Checkers. "I just want to say this right now, that regardless of what they say about it, we're going to keep it."

This was just the preliminary. People who think they remember the "Checkers speech" forget what came next. Having mawkishly bared his soul, the beleaguered candidate now took advantage of the credibility he had gained. The main thrust was counterattack. Rather than be nailed on the defensive, he dictated terms to his accusers.

"Now I am going to suggest some courses of conduct. First of all, you have read in the papers about other funds. Now, Mr. Stevenson had a *couple*. I think what Mr. Stevenson shoud do is come before the American people as I have, give the names of the people that have contributed to that fund, give the names of the people who put this money into their pockets at the same time they were receiving money from the state government, and see what favors, if any, they gave out for that."

Now to his Vice-Presidential opponent. "As far as Mr. Sparkman [Senator John J. Sparkman of Alabama] I would suggest the same thing. He's had his wife on the payroll. I don't condemn him for that. But I think he should come before the American people and indicate what outside sources of income he has had."

Nixon turned the issue from impropriety to the candidates' willingness to disclose. By undergoing the humiliation of a body frisk, he made financial disclosure a standard for office. In that competition, Nixon had finished the race before the others had left the starting gate.

The spin now had reached full torque. "I would suggest

that under the circumstances both Mr. Sparkman and Mr. Stevenson should come before the American people, as I have, and make a complete statement as to their financial history. If they don't, it will be an admission that they have something to hide."

Something to hide! At this point, General Eisenhower, watching the broadcast in Cleveland, jabbed his pencil into the legal pad he was using to take notes. This Nixon character was talking about *him!* If candidates were expected to make their taxes and other papers public, that would include Ike's own tricky finances, particularly the special legislation Congress had passed shielding from taxes the income he was still receiving from his wartime memoirs. And now here was his running mate threatening to splash the whole thing onto the front pages.

The next morning the great man met his new, hardball friend in West Virginia and declared, "You're my boy!"

The Checkers episode demonstrated that when you establish credibility, you gain control of the story and can spin it anyway you want.

Nobody has done this better than the media mavens at the Reagan White House during his politically brilliant first term. A case in point: the David A. Stockman affair of 1981.

Throughout the year, the new Administration had repudiated Democratic charges that its fiscal policy would lead to huge deficits and that its tax policies were skewed toward the rich. Then the December *Atlantic Monthly* published a long interview with David Stockman in which the Budget Director admitted in effect that the Democrats were right. Here was the President's own fiscal architect saying that the Reagan tax cut of 1981 "didn't quite mesh" with the Administration's huge Pentagon buildup. "The pieces were moving on independent tracks—the tax program, where we were going on spending, and the defense program, which was just a bunch of numbers written on a piece of paper," the Director of the Budget told the interviewer, William Greider.

The whole issue of deficits, Stockman brazenly acknowledged, had been swept under the rug by an accounting dodge the boys at the Office of Management and Budget liked to call the "magic asterisk." The only reason the Administration had for believing the deficits would be cut, in other words, was the Budget Director's bookkeeping notation that the reductions would be *announced by the President at some later date!* In other words, Fly now, pay later. In truth, the Budget Director had no idea how the deficits were going to come down: "None of us really understands what's going on with all these numbers."

So much for this "conservative" Administration's credibility on the deficit question.

Stockman's disclosures about tax policy were even more embarrassing. For months the President had maintained that his tax-cut bill was eminently fair, that its purpose was to give the average taxpayers something more to take home in their weekly paychecks. But critics were firing away, contending that the whole bill was tilted toward the rich. Now Stockman was feeding them ammunition. The real goal of the President's tax plan, he said, was to cut the very top bracket from 70 percent to 50 percent. The cuts for those in the middle-income bracket were included "in order to make this palatable as a political matter." The whole bill was simply a "Trojan horse to bring down the top rate."

It was this last metaphor that gripped the country's attention in the publicity that followed.

To control the public-relations damage, White House chief of staff James Baker choreographed a brilliant spin. The dance was a traditional two-step: first, admit you have a problem, thereby establishing credibility; then use the enhanced credibility to define the problem in a way that keeps the political damage to a minimum.

And it was Stockman himself who gave the plan the necessary packaging. According to the Budget Director's memoirs, he was called into Baker's office and told that he had one chance to keep his post. "You're going to have lunch with the President. The menu is humble pie. You're going to eat every last motherfucking spoonful of it. You're going to be the most contrite sonofabitch this world has ever seen."

Most important, he was to display this mournful pose to the White House press corps. "When you go through the Oval Office door, I want to see that sorry ass of yours dragging on the carpet."

As an insider of the Reagan White House, Stockman knew the importance that the President's advisers attached to such imagery. He knew that it was his use of the "Trojan horse" phrase that gave the original story so much life. Having gotten himself into trouble with a figure of speech, he now took the same way out.

As a child of the Minnesota farm country, he had some clever imagery on hand. "If they [the Reagan PR advisers] didn't know the difference between reality and a metaphor, I would have to give them what they wanted. A counter-metaphor. A *woodshed* story. A self-inflicted public humiliation." Stockman told the press he had been taken to the woodshed. He had been given an emotional dressing-down by his boss and father figure, the President of the United States.

So went the Washington chorus. In one small but elegant bit of stagecraft, the West Wing PR folks, running with Stockman's naughty-boy metaphor, shifted the entire media focus from an earth-shaking revelation of unsound public finance to a small soap opera: the betrayal by one bright young man of his trusting mentor.

The spin's rationale was compelling. Revelation could be dealt with only by denial. Stockman refused to make such a denial; he had been quoted accurately. It was vital, therefore, that the issue be shifted to that of betrayal. The solution to betrayal is expiation; hence the woodshed. To mass, uninformed and unanalytical audiences, the moral imagery always outdazzles the scientific.

The White House press corps fell for it. Pat Oliphant and company had been provided the perfect premise for an editorial cartoon, and they seized it. There was the little farm boy, little Davy Stockman, walking gingerly from the ominous little building, where a stern pa stood brandishing his instrument of punishment. The tears flowed from the lad's eyes, and the reader's own eyes were drawn to the caption: "A Visit to the Woodshed."

Within days, the spin had taken complete control. Of course, there were a few stories about the economic significance of Stockman's disclosures, but these were buried back in the financial sections. It was the woodshed angle that made the evening news and the front pages of the paper. By admitting that the Stockman caper represented a serious breach of loyalty—not much of an admission at this point—the Reagan team shifted attention to an issue they could manage. They even succeeded in winning the President some points for being (a) stern and (b) forgiving. The Prodigal Son was back working for the old man again, a little humbler, a little more appreciative of his father's charitable nature. Betrayal had led to punishment, contrition, and, finally, absolution.

There are few people or organizations who cannot make use of this technique at some crisis. In legal terms, putting the spin on an issue is basically an exercise in plea bargaining. Faced with an indictment, the attorney tells his client to plead guilty—but to a lower charge. In Stockman's case, we were told the crime had been personal, not fiscal. What he had done wrong was betray the trust of his political master, a deed for which he had been duly chastised.

It is a fact of human life that one's accusers can keep only a single idea in their heads at any given time. They are determined to prove your guilt, but worried that it will never be the kind of clear-cut denouement we see in a courtroom drama. Only on *Perry Mason,* it seems, does the guilty party stand up in court and scream out his crime.

The joy of spin lies in telling the accuser he is dead right and then getting the personal satisfaction of delineating exactly what he is right about.

In 1987, Jesse Jackson showed how it's done.

Speaking to an elite black-tie fund-raising audience in Washington, D.C., he paid tribute to Senator Bill Bradley of New Jersey. Jackson said that Bradley was one of his personal heroes "because of his fight against racial stereotyping. Bill Bradley triumphed against great odds to become a basketball star. He had to reach these goals despite the handicap of race and family background. We all know the Bill Bradley story: how the young white man from the right side of the tracks came to one day become a professional basketball player.

"His neighbors were riding him, and his friends laughed at him, but he persevered. Bill was determined to succeed until at last he broke the chains of race-conscious behavior to join the front ranks in the great American sport of basketball." The crowd, still giddy at the subject matter, was beginning to erupt.

"When Bill first spoke his dream out loud, his guidance counselors at school tried to discourage him, to break his spirit. Finally one of them took him aside and told him the facts of life: 'Bill, you must accept the fact that it's got nothing to do with your ability. It doesn't matter how many points you score or how loud the cheers are. You can't go to the top, because you are *white.'* "

As Jackson spoke this last, blunt word the audience of establishment Democrats went stone silent. The candidate had accomplished his dramatic objective. He was admitting that he faced tremendous odds in his campaign for President. But he was saying that the problem was not his radical positions or his devisive statements but his race, pure and simple.

It was a masterful bit of spin. The well-heeled crowd walked out of the Hilton that night thinking that Jackson had told a great joke with an ironic premise. But he had done more than that. He had laid the conceptual foundation for his second campaign for the Presidency. Sure, he had a vulnerability as a candidate, but he, Jesse Jackson, could not be blamed for that vulnerability.

Beneath the applause and the lingering titters, there was a guilty suspicion that the candidate was right.

Chapter Twelve

"The press is the enemy"

Never forget that reporters serve their apprenticeships on the night desk. When a grisly murder or auto accident occurs, it is the cub reporter, the peachy-keen Jimmy Olsen type, who drives out to the house of the freshly deceased to ask for a "recent picture" and, having made the loathsome request, stands nonchalantly in the hallway while the bereaved roots through the family albums.

The first thing to keep in mind about members of the Fourth Estate is that the people you are dealing with have passed through this journalistic boot camp. The freshly scrubbed reporters who came back with the snapshot are the hungry ones—the ones who move on to cover the living.

If that seems less than charitable, so be it. This book is not written for journalism students but for those who have to deal with them once they reach the streets.

You may be one of those cocky types who watch some business guy getting fried to a crisp on *60 Minutes* and wonder why anyone with a brain larger than a moth's would consent to be interviewed. How could someone smart enough to run a business or even a middle-sized scam still fall for such a setup? My reaction is more sympathetic. How many rolls of tape must the producers waste, I ask myself, how many softballs must be thrown, how many hours of amiable schmoozing with the victim's newfound friend Mike or Ed or Diane must be endured to warm the stooge up before letting loose with the zinger?

Fact: the higher you go in business, the more time you will spend standing blindfolded on the media firing line. You will get a taste of what politicians must endure every day of their working lives.

Pols have something to teach in this regard. As a group they may be dismissed as publicity seekers; the good ones never forget that careers can be broken more easily than made by the press. As we saw in an earlier chapter, "Tail-gunner Joe" McCarthy became a modern American demagogue playing to the hour-by-hour habits and competitive job pressures of the Capitol Hill reporter. Ronald Reagan, too, has made masterly use of the media. But, as witnessed on many an evening news program, Reagan also knew the iron rule "Only talk when it improves the silence." Striding cinematically across the South Lawn, he passed harmlessly by a whole cowpen of TV reporters and cameramen. Smiling jauntily, his hand cupped to his good ear, he strained to hear the distant shouted questions. As the mad whirl of the helicopter blades grew deafening, he shook his head, lipsynched a "Sorry, fellas" for cameras, and swaggered his way aboard *Marine One*, off to Camp David or Santa Barbara, well out of harm's way.

Many people reach a level of professional or corporate responsibility where it becomes their interest to meet the press, but not everyone can tote a helicopter around to provide the foil for such easy getaways, It is here that they should remember the somewhat hyperbolic but useful rule made famous by Richard Nixon: *The press is the enemy*.

This may seem harsh to some, and so to those gentler

ears let me put the admonition more mildly: Always remember what these people do for a living. Their mission
is to produce a good story, and in their business it's generally the bad news that makes the best headlines. Failure,
misery, disaster—that's what makes the bells go off in a
journalist's nervous system: the kind of story where somebody gets hurt.

Consider this gallery of horrors:

In July 1986, White House chief of staff Donald Regan
was briefing the press on Administration South African
policy, a touchy subject. For months the Administration
had defied the pressure from Congress and the public and
stubbornly fought economic sanctions against Pretoria.
Regan tried to send a message about the various unex-
plored consequences to our own country of such an embargo. "Are the women of America," he asked, "prepared
to give up all their jewelry?"

Don Regan is no fool. He was speaking rhetorically of
the unpublicized economic consequences of an embargo.
Furthermore, the press session was conducted under strict
ground rules. The White House staff briefing was explicitly billed as "on background." Reporters who attended could attribute remarks in general references—to
"Administration officials," for example—but not to Mr.
Regan personally.

Unfortunately for the man from Merrill Lynch, such
ground rules are not written in cement. There are loop-
holes, exceptional cases in which no matter what guide-
lines have been set, a reporter may claim the right to
ignore them.

The morning following the briefing, *Los Angeles Times*
reporter Karen Tumulty came up to my desk in the giant
Speaker's rooms of the Capitol, read me the Regan quote
from a United Press International account and said that,
based upon a later reference in the story, everyone had a

pretty good idea of which "high Administration official" had said it. Recognizing the men's-locker-room idiom favored by the chief of staff, I said, "That sounds like Diamond Don Regan."

There was blood in the water. Helen Thomas, the veteran UPI correspondent, soon changed her attribution from "high Administration" to "Don Regan." There was no point in maintaining a technical compliance with the ground rules, particularly on the part of a reporter who had not attended the briefing.

The sobriquet "Diamond Don" became a crown of thorns for the man who had been acting for months as a kind of American Prime Minister. Charges of sexism and racial insensitivity were only the beginning. Garry Trudeau's comic strip, *Doonesbury*, made Diamond Don a featured character.

How could a shrewd businessman like Don Regan expose himself to such ridicule? There are a number of explanations. One, the press that covered Wall Street, particularly in Regan's high-flying days, was far more deferential than those who chronicle the daily foibles of public officials. Two, the reporter who broke the story had not attended Regan's South Africa briefing and was therefore not bound by the ground rules. She had simply heard about the briefing, knew who conducted it, and read what was said. The ground rules could have been discarded for another reason as well: at the personal judgment by any reporter present that the remarks on women's concern for "their jewelry" were grossly sexist. Many reporters simply do not honor "on background" protection in such cases.

No matter how intricate or sophisticated the ground rules you establish with a reporter, they apply only as long as it accords with both parties' mutual interest. There is no law that says journalists need to honor the deal with a source. If the story is hot enough, ways can be found to get around any agreement. A reporter can often find an alternative source for information given to him or her off the record. "If it's on the record," Washington attorney Sven Holmes, a veteran of many Democratic campaigns, has noted, "it will appear the next day. If it's off the record, it'll run the next week."

For anyone who doubts this, think of all the times you have heard a distraught public figure try to defend himself for an ill-considered public comment by saying, "But that was off the record." Claiming "off the record" is like a defendant in a larceny case claiming entrapment. To the layman, both come across as admissions of guilt. Translation: Okay, so I said it. I didn't think it would ever make it into print.

No party has a monopoly on bloopers.

The week before Gary Hart announced for President in 1986, a key aide was quoted in *Newsweek* on his candidate's private life: "He's always in jeopardy of having the sex issue raised if he can't keep his pants on."

When the aide called Colorado in an attempt to explain his remark to the campaigning Harts, the candidate's wife was overheard saying, "Tell him to save his dime." The following week, *Newsweek* carried a letter from the unhappy man, under the headline "A Clarification on Hart." The aide began by saying that he had understood the pain-causing interview to be off the record. "The particular quote attributed to me was made in a speculative and purely hypothetical context," he continued, "contrary to the actual facts as I know them." The damage had been done, to the candidate and to the relationship. Far worse damage would be done, of course, when the candidate was found in the same compromising position his aide had feared.

To sum up, there are only two kinds of media-wise politicians: those who are born fearing the press—who keep their distance from day one—and those who learn to fear it the hard way.

One more for the books: the great burlesque tale of "How Earl Became the Butz of his own Joke."

In the days just after the 1976 Republican national convention, President Ford's Agriculture Secretary was flying westward to visit a screwworm-eradication plant in Mexico, which in hindsight seems a grotesquely appropriate destination. Riding in the first-class compartment of a commercial airline, Earl Butz spotted singers Pat Boone and Sonny Bono. With them was John Dean, the former White House counsel and Watergate whistle-blower, in his most recent incarnation: as a reporter back from covering the Republican convention for *Rolling Stone.*

After some introductory towel-snapping, the conversation turned to politics, and Pat Boone asked the Secretary of Agriculture why so few blacks were drawn to the Republican Party.

Butz replied, "The only things that coloreds are looking for in life are tight pussy, loose shoes and a warm place to shit."

Dean obviously shared Butz's sense that it was too good a line to be wasted. He included it in his article for *Rolling Stone,* attributing it to a "member of the Ford cabinet." Dean's story mentioned that the barnyard slur was made on a plane heading west following Ford's nomination, and by elimination *New Times,* a competing magazine, nailed Butz as the flying Cabinet comedian. You have to wonder what inner demon had lulled him into telling a racist joke in the presence of an aspiring political journalist who three years earlier had sold out his President.

Unfortunately, anyone involved in press relations must, to use the phrase made famous by Hollywood publicity man Harry Rogers, "walk the tightrope." You must be bold and dramatic enough to get your message across—always in competition with millions of others—without plunging to your death.

To protect yourself, here are a handful of terms that might keep you balanced:

When you speak on "background," that means the reporter cannot quote you by name. But it does not constrain him or her from describing you in such a way—"a key aide to the Speaker" or "someone who works closely with the plant manager"—as to cause almost as much trouble as your name itself.

"Deep background" applies when you want the reporter to publish or broadcast the information, but not attributed in any way that could even vaguely identify you. Such was the agreement Carl Bernstein and Bob Woodward made with their Watergate source "Deep Throat." When you read a story that includes the phrase "sources said," you know you're reading a story put out on deep background.

"Off the record" means that the reporter cannot use the information. It can do handstands in a reporter's head; it can be indispensable in making sense of other matters; it may govern the tone in which crucial issues are reported; but it can't appear in print.

None of these ground rules should ever be presumed. Reporters are not required to read you your Miranda rights. They don't have to tell you that you are on the record. That's the assumption.

Being conversant with the various types of ground rules is hardly enough. You need to use them *explicitly*. Politicians and their spokesmen, anyone who works regularly with the press, must develop for their own survival a mental set of *stoppers* that will force them to say, "Now, this is on background, okay?" "Now, I don't want this identified as a 'Democratic aide,' 'leadership aide' or anything like that, okay?"

Never forget, in using such lingo you are always treading the edge of disaster. Ground rules are made by the players and for the players. If you enjoy a relationship of ongoing trust with journalists, these ground rules can benefit both of you. A good reporter will respect such arrangements, not just for ethical reasons but because he or she doesn't want to dry up a good source or gain a bad reputation.

But the minute one side doesn't want to play that way anymore, he or she can simply end the game. Reporters may use what they have available at any moment, out of a ruthless calculation that what has been obtained from you is more important than anything you might provide in the future. You should be particularly fearful of any reporter who urges you to tell him something off the record. If he cannot use the information, why does he want it?

The best rule to remember here is this: Don't do the crime if you can't do the time. If having your words appear in the *Wall Street Journal* could cost you your job, it is foolhardy to go "on background." If the downside is simply a bad day or two at the office, and you trust the reporter to stick to the ground rules, why not? Life is short. Have some fun.

Even so, it's a good idea to keep your wits about you even when dealing with genuinely good friends in the press. Like policemen, they are always on duty. This goes double for "social occasions." Anything you say after a few drinks is as good as something you said during the press briefing or on the subway on the way to work. As White House press aide Larry Speakes once told his troops, "You may get a free dinner tonight, but you will regret it in the morning."

Even under the tightest ground rules, some things you tell the press will always be fair game. One category includes anything that might be even broadly taken as an ethnic slur.

As some will remember, in 1984 Jesse Jackson, candidate for President, had a casual conversation with a group of black reporters in which he referred to Jews and New York City as "Hymie" and "Hymietown." The next weekend, the *Washington Post* broke this in a major story. Jackson's defense was that he had premised his remarks by saying, "Let's talk *black* talk." But his claim to privacy is disqualified on two accounts: one, he failed to get an explicit off-the-record agreement from the reporters; two, his remarks fit into the category of ethnic slurs. Many reporters simply consider such comments an abuse of their confidence.

Like it or not, we live in the "Gotcha!" era of journalism. If a reporter can nail you in the process of nailing down his story, he will.

These are tough challenges for those who have to make their living in press relations. Stories need to be interesting, but not too interesting. I know all too well the sound of the *Washington Post* and the *New York Times* hitting the lawn after a sleepless night spent wondering whether I had gone far enough to get quoted but not far enough to get burned. "I have been right and I have been paranoid," former Nixon aide and now columnist William Safire once said, "and it's better being paranoid."

I first learned the perils of "Gotcha!" journalism while working the other side of the reporter's notebook. At the end of 1973 I was congressional correspondent for a small news service in Washington underwritten by Ralph Nader. Nixon had just carried out the "Saturday Night Massacre," and Woodward and Bernstein were blazing hot. "Investigative" journalism was coming into fashion. Everyone was digging for the next big story of evil, corruption or anything that would embarrass the powerful. I remember trying to file my story one night as Peter Gruenstein, the bureau chief, paced through the office smoking a cigar and repeating over and over, *"Dirt. We've got to find some dirt."* When I wrote a standard, informative news story, it was dismissed as routine. "Press-release stuff," Gruenstein would grumble.

After several weeks of dry holes, I came up with a story that met the chief's standard. A former aide to a Pennsylvania congressman had some "dirt" for me. It involved his old boss in a classic conflict of interest. For years the Congressman had carried on his House of Representatives payroll a reporter who also covered the Congressman for a local newspaper. Every month the reporter had received two paychecks: one from his paper, the other from his friendly legislator down in Washington.

When I called the newspaper's managing editor, he said he knew about the moonlighting but denied any conflict. The way he saw it, the role of journalist and publicist complemented each other. "Whenever Joe does anything, our reporter's right on top of it."

Soon thereafter, I stopped the Congressman in the Speaker's Lobby of the House to get his reaction. "Worst story in ten years." Of course it was. Before I came along, he was used to seeing only his own press releases in the local papers.

But in fact he had a point. Under the old rules, the little arrangement was tacitly acceptable. It wasn't long ago, after all, that a politician didn't even have to put a reporter on the payroll to be sure of getting kid-glove treatment. If you bought the guy a beer, you figured you owned him. In those old days of flagrant newspaper partisanship, fueled on anything from religious prejudice to advertising contracts, there were two kinds of reporters: yours and theirs. You trusted yours and you stiffed theirs.

Today it is much harder to tell who your friends are.

Early in 1984, a reporter called about a story he was doing for the up-scale men's magazine *M*. He wanted to focus on a handful of Capitol Hill staffers and asked whether he should do it on me or on the Speaker's general counsel, Kirk O'Donnell. In hindsight I should have passed this golden opportunity to my colleague. The piece made it appear not that I worked for the Speaker but the other way around. I can quote one line from memory: "Everyone in Washington who is anyone knows how Christopher Matthews guides the Speaker of the House." *Guides?* Advises, okay. Counsels, sure, but *guides?*

The article did not play well. Tip O'Neill told me face to face what he thought of the piece. It would have done little good at that particular moment to point out that the offending line had not even been written by the interviewer but by an editor, dashing off an introduction to the article.

Unfortunately, this was not the end of it. Several weeks later after drinks and dinner at our house, then some after-dinner drinks, I was sitting at a long dining-room table with columnist Nicholas von Hoffman and another journalist. We were talking about the relationship between reporters and the people they cover. "Believe me," my friend Nick implored, "there's no such thing as off the record. Don't trust *anyone*."

Ignoring the warning, I acknowledged that my boss, Tip O'Neill, was not at all happy with the *M* portrait of me as his Svengali.

I should have listened to Nick. Going on that late-night rumination, my other late-night journalist buddy reported in the weekly newspaper he edited that I was on the verge of being fired.

Don't trust any of them. Always remember: they're wired to a different system from yours. They become physically aroused when you say things to them that will cause you or someone else immeasurable grief. You can see it sometimes in the slight flicker their eyelids make when you say something *interesting*. It is at that instant, already too late, that you remember that these were the boys and girls who many a dreary afternoon ago came back radiantly clutching that tear-stained snapshot.

Chapter Thirteen

The Reputation of Power

> The reputation of power is power.
>   —THOMAS HOBBES

Spending my summers as a youth doing odd jobs at the New Jersey shore, I worked for the Murray brothers. Bernie, the older of the two, had spent twenty-nine years as a roustabout for Barnum and Bailey, moving from city to city, consuming a fifth of hard liquor a day. When I knew him, he had given it all up—the circus, the traveling, the booze—and was painting houses in Ocean City, taking time out every hour for a cup of coffee to make up for the alcohol his body still craved.

Bernie may have tamed the carny restlessness, drowned the carny thirst, but he had kept the carny attitude. While he and his actively alcoholic brother, Joe, made a small living brightening up the old Victorian seashore homes, he would occasionally revert to the lingo of the big top. "Let's Wabash this and get out of here," he'd say as the late-afternoon shadows started to cross the porch we were too slowly finishing.

To "Wabash" meant to drown the paint in thinner, miraculously giving wings to the brushes, which had been dragging along the railings and the pillars. The completed surface glistened. In minutes the task of hours was over, and weeks later, when a gloss that was meant for years began to peel and fade, the Murray brothers were working another part of town.

There's a lot of Wabashing in politics. It's no accident that the organizers of political campaigns and the promoters of circus tours are both called advance men. They arrive, build the ballyhoo, and leave town just ahead of the menagerie.

It's also fair to say that a great deal of reputation-building rests on Wabashing. It is very often based less on reality than on appearance, on making people do things they don't want to do by making them think they want to do them. As Harry Truman put it, "A leader is a man who has the ability to get other people to do what they don't want to do and like it."

With some exceptions—J. Edgar Hoover, Richard Daley, Huey Long come to mind—most political leaders lack raw political clout. They cannot, fortunately, have their opponents beheaded. Neither can they make their idiot relatives into dukes and earls. In a democratic society, leaders wield a different sort of authority: they become powerful by *appearing* powerful, and studying them reveals a number of tricks valuable to those who would seek power in any profession.

Play your strengths.

During the 1982 political season, pollster Peter Hart told congressional Democrats to emphasize issues like the economy and Social Security. The more they got such issues into the headlines, the better they did in the polls. Conversely, he warned the party leadership to stay away from the budget issue. Say what they might about the growing deficits under the new Administration, Democrats simply were not credible on fiscal responsibility. People thought of them as spending too much money and raising taxes too high.

President Reagan's pollsters must have been telling him the same thing. The White House staff did everything they could to focus attention on the budget issue. In 1982 the

President came to Capitol Hill for a "budget summit" with the congressional leaders of both parties, bringing with him a huge White House press corps and its vast array of TV cameramen and still photographers. For two hours, the Chief Executive met with the leadership in what was to be a cavalcade of public relations. The President and the Congress had not reached agreement in more than a year; they were not going to get further in two hours.

The real action was outside the room. With the thousand-strong press corps packed behind security ropes, White House press spokesman Larry Speakes moved among them, throwing out news morsels like a trainer feeding the dolphins at Sea World. The President's decision to "walk the extra mile" to find an agreement was going to pay big dividends on the evening news.

Merely by moving the regular weekly meeting between the President and the Congress from the White House to the Capitol, Reagan's PR gurus had made the same old story of fiscal politics into a big item for the networks.

The results followed the script exactly. "Budget" became a term of major journalistic importance. The President was seen to be "doing something" about the deficit. To make sure no one missed the imagery, the White House added numbers to the picture. Chief of staff Jim Baker held a full-scale briefing at 5 P.M., just in time for the evening news, just in time to put the right spin on the story: Congress was just sitting on its collective duff; Reagan was *trying*, at least.

And how it paid off. While the "budget summit" of 1982 did not reduce the deficit by a cent, it won tremendous points for Reagan on the tube. His pollsters had tagged the budget issue as a winner for Republicans. So long as the word "budget" appeared in the headlines, the GOP regained support. It didn't much matter what was happening to the budget—in this case, nothing at all—so long as it was being talked about.

But two can play the same game. On the eve of the '82 elections, it was Democrats who pulled the stunt. A week before the balloting I called Spencer Rich of the *Washington Post* with a story I had picked up that the Administration was planning some post-election changes in the politically volatile Social Security program.

While he refused to bite at the sugarplum I was selling, Rich had something even tastier on his plate: he had gotten word that the National Republican Congressional Campaign Committee had sent out an embarrassing fundraising letter on the very same matter, Social Security, and he wondered whether I knew how to get hold of it.

I did. Eric Berkman a real starker over at the Democrats' own campaign committee could dig up anything, particularly what we like to call "negative research."

Sure enough, the Republican fund-raisers had recently asked potential contributors to "vote" by choosing among several "ballots" for their preferred solution to the current Social Security funding crisis. "Ballot A" called for making Social Security "voluntary." For the GOP candidates that fall, it might as well have been a suicide note.

The next morning, the Thursday before the nation's senior citizens and their younger sympathizers cast their real ballots, Spencer Rich's article ran on the inside pages of the *Post*. The position and the play given the story were extremely low-key and nonpolitical.

But that was merely the crack of the starter's gun. By 9 A.M. the Speaker had issued a written statement demanding that "President Reagan personally condemn the Republicans' suggestion that Social Security be made voluntary."

The story moved immediately on United Press International. Within hours, the President arrived for his last campaign swing through Wyoming, to be confronted by a posse of wire reporters. Did he or did he not agree with the GOP letter?

Reagan was furious, denying any suggestion that he intended to tamper with Social Security. Politically, however, the damage was done. The man who had been haunted his entire career by an early suggestion that "voluntary features be introduced into the Social Security program" was spinning his wheels in the rut.

Rule: *When you're in a hole, stop digging.* Just as the Republicans were smart to play up the budget as a no-lose issue, they were stupid to continue harping on the Social Security question. The more they did, the weaker they appeared.

There's a great old political story passed down over the years: An elderly woman tells a reporter that she intends to vote against Senator Barry Goldwater, the 1964 Republican candidate for President: "He's the guy who's going to get rid of TV."

"But, madam," interrupts the reporter, "I think you're making a mistake. Senator Goldwater is talking about getting rid of the Tennessee Valley Authority, TVA."

"Well," the elderly woman persists, "I'm not taking any chances."

As we saw earlier, it is important to admit your failings —not in order to gain ground on your opponent, but to put the issue behind you. Having admitted your weaknesses and your opponent's strengths, the only things left to debate are your strengths and your opponent's weaknesses.

Lowballing.

Here is a classic example of the sort of public-relations foreplay that politicians can teach their fellow citizens. The concept is clear enough: the best way to impress the fans with your slam-dunking ability is to set the basket at eight feet instead of the regulation ten. Watching you stuff the ball through that secretly stunted hoop, the folks at home will think it's Wilt Chamberlain out there.

In 1968, at the height of the Vietnam War, Eugene

McCarthy, then a relatively unknown United States senator from Minnesota, beat President Lyndon Johnson in the
New Hampshire primaries. It was that come-from-behind
defeat that brought Senator Robert F. Kennedy into the
race and drove Johnson to announce his retirement a few
weeks later.

Now, that is what people *think* happened in the political
snows of '68. What really happened is quite different. Lyndon Johnson not only won the New Hampshire primary of
that year, he did it without campaigning and without even
having his name appear on the ballot. Voters going to the
polls had to write in LBJ's name, and despite that incon-
venience, despite a sharp inflation and a terrible war, he
still went on to beat McCarthy, a man who had been campaigning in the state for months. But the press was fixed
on the idea that if the apparently academic Midwesterner
gleaned a substantial vote against the incumbent President, that was tantamount to victory. McCarthy's losing
vote of 42 percent surpassed these expectations. The press
became so intoxicated with the David-and-Goliath angle
of the contest that they could not bring themselves to score
the victory when it actually went to Goliath.

As we see in this case, lowballing is a blunter cousin of
spin. Mondale "won" Super Tuesday because his campaign manager had sold the media on the notion that sur-
viving and winning were tantamount to the same thing.
McCarthy "beat" LBJ back in '68 because he simply managed to set a low level of expectations. Spin is a curve ball.
Lowballing is more like a fast ball. If you throw the message hard enough, it'll get past just enough of the batters
for you to win.

Four years later, in the same New Hampshire primary,
Edmund Muskie defeated George McGovern 46 percent
to 37 percent. The press declared McGovern the victor. A
prime reason was that a Muskie campaign worker had fool-

ishly said, "If we don't get fifty percent, I'll slit my throat."
McGovern's people were far smarter. By presenting their
candidate to primary voters as the antiwar idealist and pic-
turing Muskie as the prisoner of the political center,
McGovern's people built the notion that their man could
claim victory if he won any sizable vote whatsoever. After
all, he was not really playing the usual political game of
going for the center.

By the 1980 primary season, lowballing had become an
art form. Faced with a challenge for the nomination by
Senator Edward Kennedy, President Carter sent his people off to work the Iowa caucuses, where Carter had scored
such an impressive vote four years earlier. A seasoned Carter press spokesman, Edward Jesser, had a particular mission: to convince the traveling political press corps that
Ted Kennedy had it wrapped up in the Hawkeye State.

As caucus day approached, the conventional wisdom
had it that Ted Kennedy "had the best organization on the
ground ever seen in Iowa," a phrase beautifully concocted
by Jesser, whose weeks of drinking with reporters and be-
moaning the strengths of the Kennedy effort were triumphantly paying off.

When Carter eventually beat Kennedy by a ratio of three
to one, it blew the Last Brother so far out of the race that
he was forced to give a major campaign address at Georgetown University which transformed a serious try for the
Presidency to a last hurrah for liberalism. The man who
two weeks before was the favored national candidate was
forced to offer himself as a forlorn idealist, a late-model
Adlai Stevenson.

Jesser, the man who did more than anyone else to jack
up false expectations of a Kennedy juggernaut, returned
East, dispensing his legendary farewell to the land of
wheat and corn, "Will the last person leaving Des Moines
please turn out the lights?"

A few months later, I took leave from the White House to serve as Carter campaign spokesman in the Pennsylvania primary with an assignment similar to Jesser's in Iowa: to play the expectations game, convincing the press that even if Kennedy won the state it was no big deal. After all, the challenger had spent a tremendous amount of time there and pushed all the right buttons politically—paying a courtesy call on Cardinal Krol, eating Philadelphia soft pretzels on Broad Street, doubling up on the radio call-in shows. Carter, meanwhile, was following his "Rose Garden strategy" of staying in the White House and tending to the Iran hostage crisis.

Lowballing came easy here. People already believed that Carter was going to do badly. He had lost the big primary in neighboring New York, an awkward and visible sign of the nation's dismay at his inability to free the Americans held by the crazed "students" in Teheran. The real campaign was being waged by the crowd in Iran, with Carter losing it. But some people could still see straight. When I attempted to lowball Carter's chances in Pennsylvania, Robert Shogen of the *Los Angeles Times* had had enough of it. "I've known people who have said they are going to lose and they *still* lost," he said.

Nevertheless it worked. Buoyed by Jerry Rafshoon's brilliant and devastating man-in-the-street TV ads, which painfully exposed Kennedy's personal problems, Carter barely lost the state. Because the vote count was extremely close and took much of the night, the challenger did not even "win" in the first editions. The *Philadelphia Daily News*, a tabloid, filled its entire front page with one word: "Squeaker!" That was the best Carter could have hoped for. Kennedy, the man who was supposed to win by divine right, had gotten caught in a stalemate.

Ronald Reagan made a career of such tricks. He lowballed his opponents longer than anyone can remember.

Playing the aw-shucks average citizen standing up to the government and the political establishment, he did the road show of *Mr. Smith Goes to Washington* almost as many times as that great old movie has been revived. As Governor Edmund G. "Pat" Brown, the man he beat in 1966, once wrote, "In continuing to call himself an amateur or 'citizen' politician, Reagan applies the same logic the Soviets do when they declare their Olympic athletes to be amateurs despite overwelming evidence to the contrary."

At each stage of his career, Reagan let the press, the public and, most important, his opponents believe that there is less there than meets the eye. When Reagan ran for governor the first time, the incumbent's people felt they could easily handle the "ex–movie actor." In 1980, the Carter people thought his background would make him the easiest opponent to defeat. When Reagan was inaugurated, he was greeted by Speaker O'Neill with the words "Welcome to the major leagues, Mr. President." As the years of partisan combat lengthened, both men would reappraise their original estimates. Tip O'Neill would recognize a brilliant media-age politician. Reagan would see the Speaker's Harris Poll figures climb to 65 percent at a time when his own fell below 50 percent.

Every businessman knows the importance of setting modest projections for sales and output. Just as a baseball team that finishes in the cellar has nowhere to go but up, so a firm that is bumping along below the zero line is exactly the kind of executive opportunity an eager beaver should want. In any profession, the lower the threshold of success, the greater the chances for success. As the young Winston Churchill discovered in his early political career, the worst thing a politician can do is promise something he cannot deliver. In World War II, he gave the worst-case scenario to the British people. Following the British evacuation of Dunkirk, he gave what might have been his finest speech.

Imagining a Nazi invasion of England, Churchill promised that his countrymen would "fight on the beaches . . . on the landing grounds . . . in the streets . . . in the hills . . . We shall never surrender. Even if," he continued, "which I do not for a moment believe, this island, or a large part of it, were subjugated and starving, then our empire beyond the seas . . . would carry on the struggle, until, in God's good time, the New World, with all its power and might, steps forth to the rescue and liberation of the Old."

There was romance in those words, but brilliant politics as well. In suggesting the very worst, the wartime Prime Minister was ensuring his own government a sufficient claim on British patience. Battles might still be lost, because the people were prepared to endure the worst.

The smartest thing anyone in a position of responsibility can do is pick a modest short-term goal, in this case avoiding annihilation of the British Commonwealth. Once he has delivered on this goal, he can proceed steadily to even greater undertakings, and triumph magnificently. As Lee Atwater, the Republican strategist who has served both Ronald Reagan and George Bush, put it, "David is *still* getting good publicity for beating Goliath."

Sandbagging.

This is the corollary of lowballing. One of the most effective means of diminishing your opponent's stature is to advertise his strengths, to set unreasonable expectations of his potential. This is how Ronald Reagan's advisers set up Jimmy Carter in the general election. The dominant issue of the campaign, as everyone remembers, was the kidnapping of fifty American diplomats in Teheran. Fearing that the incumbent might be lucky enough to spring the hostages before election day, the Reagan team revved up the rumor mill; the press and the public could expect an "October surprise." Carter and his people, Reagan headquarters muttered, had a plan to gain the Americans' release in the final month of the campaign. Had Carter succeeded he would have found the media inoculated, the political gain minimized by the imputation that the hostages had been released on a political timetable.

In the end, Carter was luckless. The hostages stayed in Teheran. It was the White House that changed hands. For those of us who recalled the "October surprise" story on election day, it was just one more insult added to the injury, one more nail in Jimmy Carter's political coffin.

The nastiest trick you can pull on any competitor is to build him up beyond his capabilities. One of the means by which Democrats maintained control of one house of Congress and recovered the other during the Reagan years was the chorus of admiration at the President's charm and communications skills. By freely admitting what a brilliant and popular "communicator" the President was, by singling out Reagan the man, they were isolating his popularity from that of his political party, cutting off his coattails. That left the Democrats holding tremendous governmental power even in a time of conservative popularity.

Readers of *The Last Hurrah* might recall a sandbagging coup of Mayor Skeffington's. To punish an old Brahmin who had fired the mayor's mother from a housekeeping job, he appoints the man's idiot son fire commissioner. Within a matter of weeks, the poor fool has become a public joke, as well as a public menace. The Irish mayor had found a way to return very publicly the humiliation that was visited on his own family by the Yankee elite a generation earlier: raw justice dispensed not by tearing down his adversary's family but by devilishly building it up.

In both lowballing and sandbagging, the principle is the same: create a handicapping system that makes any success of yours seem bigger than it is and your opponent's victory much smaller.

Creating new commandments.

When Eisenhower entered politics in 1952, he sought to maintain the aura of battlefield hero he had won as Supreme Allied Commander in World War II. As his grandson David put it many years later, it was difficult for him to be impressed with the honor of getting more votes than somebody else after having received the Nazi surrender in the Rheims cathedral.

To stay at the peak of national popularity once he was in office, Ike needed to keep himself above the tawdry bickering of intramural Republican politics. But he also faced the vexing problem of Senator Joseph R. McCarthy. McCarthy, the mad genius of public opinion, had continued his hunting of alleged Communists in government despite the transition to a Republican Presidency.

While Eisenhower eventually helped arrange the back-stage maneuvers that led to the Senator's decline, he developed a gimmick for avoiding public brawls with Tailgunner Joe. He would respond to press questions about McCarthy's escalating outrages by declaring his practice of "not engaging in personalities."

Lyndon Johnson knew the same trick. In 1964 he was confronted with what seemed the inevitable imposition of Robert Kennedy—the holdover Attorney General—as his running mate. To LBJ, this would have been a capitulation to a brutal turn of events: history would record him as the Kennedy family caretaker, a retainer who kept the seat warm until the younger brother could get into position to reclaim it. To put Bobby on the national ticket would have been tantamount to accepting a mere regent's post under the Kennedy dynasty; for a man who had long felt patronized by the late President's brother, this would have been the final humiliation. The trick was to find some way of not picking RFK and, at the same time, not offending the Kennedy family's adoring legions throughout the country.

After months of wrestling with the problem, the grumpy

Texan found his solution. He went before the White
House television cameras to announce in what became the
new standard for arbitrary commandment-creation: "I
have reached the conclusion that it would be inadvisable
for me to recommend to the convention any member of my
Cabinet or any of those who meet regularly with the Cabinet."

Washington insiders knew full well that the target of this
new precept for Vice-Presidential selection was Bobby
Kennedy and Bobby alone. The sweeping nature of
Johnson's statement had managed, however, to obscure
some of the vindictiveness of the blow. The maneuver
got the Kennedy albatross from Johnson's back for four
years.

At the outset of the 1980 Presidential election, candidate
Reagan's greatest worry was not Jimmy Carter, burdened
with inflation and the Iranian hostage situation. His problem was his own long career as a right-wing political commentator who had been unafraid to make bold but perhaps
impolitic remarks. "We should declare war on North Vietnam," he had once declaimed. "We should pave the whole
country and put parking stripes on it and still be home for
Christmas." Then, of course, there was his proposal in '64
to make Social Security "voluntary." Had his Republican
opponents gone after this baggage with any kind of gusto,
he would have been out of the race in the early going.
Even if he had won the primaries, his competitors for the
nomination would have given the Democrats so much
ammo that even a weakened Carter might have beaten him
in November.

The trick, therefore, was to keep George Bush, Howard
Baker, Bob Dole and his other opponents from getting too
tough on him. The ingenious device Reagan introduced to
the political stage was something that he liked to brandish
Moses-like as the "Eleventh Commandment: Thou shalt

not speak ill of a fellow Republican." Never mind that in 1976 Ronald Reagan had kicked the bejesus out of an incumbent Republican President of the United States to advance his own career. A cheery new dispensation was in effect. If Reagan was going to beat Carter in the fall, he needed a *bye* through the preliminary tournaments. Refusing to criticize Bush or Baker or Dole or John Connally or Phil Crane, he focused all his fire on President Carter. When his GOP competitors refused to play by the same rules, he cried foul.

Reagan pulled another commandment out of his hat in early 1987 when it came time to change chiefs of staff. Rather than ask Donald Regan to resign, he used a *photo opportunity* to tell the press that he "never talks to a person who decides to go back to private life." Instant commandment! The President's hint was hard to ignore, even by a relentlessly ambitious man like Regan. Nevertheless, it gave the Chief Executive himself a way to sidestep responsibility for Regan's resignation, which came within a matter of days.

Passing the buck.

This is the much-maligned old American expression for shifting responsibility for a tough call to someone else. President Truman added to its infamy when he placed that famous plaque on his desk reading "The Buck Stops Here."

What we tend to forget is that Give-'em-hell Harry made so many tough decisions—from dropping the atom bomb on Japan to firing General Douglas A. MacArthur—that he also made quite a few enemies. He left office with a popularity rating in the low twenties. Given his record, it is no wonder his successor in the Oval Office let Truman take that plaque back to his library in Independence.

As President, Dwight Eisenhower displayed a genius for delegation. His wartime service had taught him better than anyone else in the world how to get other people, other nations if necessary, to do his work for him. During the late 1950s, when Eisenhower's farm policies ran into trouble, it was Secretary of Agriculture Ezra Taft Benson who took the heat. The same went for foreign policy. When Ike did something unpopular abroad, Secretary of State John Foster Dulles took the flak; it was his name that people tagged with a policy reversal. And to handle his press relations Eisenhower hired the best Presidential press secretary in history, James Hagerty. On many occasions, it was Hagerty's job to serve as the White House press corps's punching bag. Here is how Hagerty himself described it:

"Eisenhower would say, 'Do it this way.' and I would say, 'If I go to the press conference and say what you want me to say, I would get hell.' With that, he would smile, get up and walk around the desk, pat me on the back and say, 'My boy, better you than me.' "

Ronald Reagan has specialized in a new form of buckpassing: the *commission*. For a man opposed to bureaucracy, he displayed a remarkable proclivity once in office for creating little boards and panels, all of them salted with Democrats, to take the heat for controversial decisions. There was the Kissinger Commission on Central America, whose job was to rationalize U.S. military aid to that region. There was the Packard Commission, to co-opt the push for defense economizing. There was the Social Security Commission, whose job was to sell the country on higher payroll taxes and a delay in cost-of-living adjustments. There was the Scowcroft Commission, to sell Congress on the MX missile. Finally there was the Tower Commission to look into the Iranian arms-for-hostages deal. Even in the latter case, Reagan was able to use the commission gambit to his advantage. The Tower Commission was mandated to focus on procedures and organizational structure, not on policy. It necessarily pointed the finger at those staff people responsible for executing policy, not at the big-picture people such as the President.

When there is no commission to take the heat, Reagan flips the hot potato to his staff. For years, the White House press corps had an infallible way to tell whether Ronald Reagan won or lost a vote on Capitol Hill. If he won, the Gipper himself would appear triumphantly in the West Wing press room, and the event would be open to full press coverage. If Reagan lost, his spokesman Larry Speakes or one of his less-known deputies would appear. In such cases, of course, no cameras would be permitted. "Success has many fathers," John F. Kennedy once said, "but failure is an orphan."

Inchon landings.

We now turn to the ultimate PR flanking maneuver. Nothing more confuses the opposition than a raid behind enemy lines. In 1950, American-led UN forces were pinned down at the bottom tip of Korea by the invading North Korean Army. Rather than fighting an inch-by-inch counterattack against hardened positions, General Douglas MacArthur executed a brilliant amphibious landing at Inchon. Within days he had recaptured Seoul; within two weeks all of South Korea had been liberated.

Like generals, politicians are remembered for their surprises. They earn particular respect when they outflank their opponents by seizing the political ground to the enemy's rear.

A wonderful example of a political Inchon landing was executed by Harry Truman. In 1948 the President looked like a loser. He arrived at the sweltering Democratic convention in Philadelphia the underdog in every poll, a man who had no prayer of election. Truman's speech, largely extemporaneous, unleashed the now famous give-'em-hell style that was to be identified with the biggest political upset in American history. Yet the real corker of the evening was not what Truman said but what he announced he was going to *do*. Reading through the list of Republican campaign promises on medical care, housing, price controls, aid to education, Truman declared that he was going to call the Republican-controlled Congress back for a special, unscheduled session to make good on their platform commitments. "Now, my friends, if there is any reality behind that Republican platform, we ought to get some action from a short session of the Eightieth Congress."

Caught totally off guard by Truman's gambit, the sulking Republicans ended up accomplishing nothing during the special two-week congressional session. As the Congress finally adjourned, Truman gave them a final punch to the midsection. He called a press conference to declare the retreating legislators the "do-nothing Congress" that had just completed its "do-nothing" session.

When America voted in November, the Democratic President managed to confound every major opinion poll and every well-known commentator in the country. By this one flanking maneuver he had put the Republicans on the defensive: instead of being in the position of national critics, they had become the incumbents, the party responsible for getting something done pronto. If they cared so much about their platform, let them pass it!

Richard Nixon pulled a similar Inchon landing in the 1970s. Throughout his career he had blistered Democrats for advocating admission of Red China to the United Nations. The mere mention of the idea got a person branded as a left-winger, "soft on Communism." In fact, no one was louder in these assaults, going back to the "Who lost China?" era, than Nixon himself. He had spent much of the 1950s blasting those who saw room for accommodation with the Chinese mainland. "I think it is wishful thinking to predict a split between Red China and the Soviet Union," he said. Yet what has secured Nixon's place in history was his decision to open the door to China in 1971.

It was his spectacular trip to Peking that year, secretly advanced by Henry Kissinger, that shocked his opponents and made believers of people who had disliked the man for decades. Richard Nixon had done something his rivals would not have dared do for fear of *Richard Nixon*.

The irony was not lost on his critics. "American conservatives, because no one doubts their hatred of Communism," the liberal economist John Kenneth Galbraith has written, "have more easily come to terms with reality and made more sensible bargainers with the Soviets and the Chinese than American liberals, who, as ever, have lived in the fear of being labeled 'soft on Communism.' " Hubert Humphrey would have been pilloried if he had traveled to Red China and stood around toasting Chou En-Lai and the rest of the gang. For Nixon, the venomous anti-Communist, the opening to "Red China" may be the one accomplishment that will salvage his public record.

Rule: To confound the competition, seize the ground behind them. Nothing spreads panic quicker than the dread realization that the enemy has penetrated your lines and is operating to your rear.

As always, the military parallel remains a strong one. During the Six-Day War in 1967, Israeli forces faked an Arab radio broadcast declaring that a key city on the road to Damascus had fallen. Hearing the phony news dispatch, frightened Syrian troops abandoned their pillboxes along the Golan Heights and began a madcap retreat.

This is one case where some well-placed PR hardball literally did the job of a howitzer.

Chapter Fourteen

Positioning

I have just thought of something that is not part of my speech, and I am worried whether I should do it.

—RONALD REAGAN

On the night of January 25, 1983, the President of the United States arrived at the Capitol to deliver his annual State of the Union address. As usual, the Speaker's office served as his holding room in the moments before he entered the House chamber. Shaking hands with the staff, he noticed Congressman Don Edwards in the room adjoining, scanning a text of the President's remarks. "How did you get that, Don?" he asked his fellow Californian, and learned for the first time that bootlegged copies of his speech text had gotten to members of Congress.

Armed with copies of the speech, Democrats on the House floor were indeed planning to bushwhack the President. They found a line in which that fiercest of Republicans seemed to admit for the first time it was the government's responsibility to do something about the towering unemployment rate. For months, Reagan had argued for "staying the course"; high unemployment rates, he promised, would be driven down by the 1981 tax cuts. Yet in his prepared text there was a line that could easily be read otherwise: "We who are in government must take the lead in restoring the economy."

The Democrats had hatched a plan. As the President

read the line, they rose in a standing ovation. For a moment Reagan seemed to be caught off guard. The message to the country was sharp and sound: they were cheering the President's grudging admission that it was up to his Administration to do something.

Reagan paused, waiting for the applause to abate, acknowledging the little tease from the Democratic back benches with a long, good-natured smile. Then, with perfect Jack Benny timing, came the haymaker: "And there all along I thought you were reading the *papers.*"

The Democrats, thinking the President was referring harmlessly to the speech texts many of them had been following and sometimes annotating for response, erupted in laughter. They had failed to see the mischief. To the people back home in their living rooms, the barb was unmistakable: the legislators were just a pack of typical, feet-up-on-the-desk, newspaper-reading, cigar-chomping pols. Reagan had got his "studio audience" to provide a laugh track for the joke of which they themselves were the butt.

A week later, he pulled a similar number, this time employing the White House press corps as his studio audience. In the midst of an afternoon press conference, his wife, Nancy, wheeled in a birthday cake. The President was seventy-two. As he cheerily began slicing pieces for all those assembled, ABC's Sam Donaldson barked out, "But you understand we won't sell out for a piece of cake. No deals."

Pause.

"Oh," the President said, looking directly at Sam, "you've sold out for less than *that.*" Donaldson's colleagues roller-coastered with laughter. Finally someone had outzinged their smart-aleck colleague.

There was another, unspoken message to those at home: the President was telling Washington reporters right to their faces that their coverage was tainted by special interests, that they are ready to be "bought": an affirmation of what right-wing critics had been saying about Big Media for decades. Not only that, but he had got them to laugh at the truth of what he was saying. As he had done on the floor of Congress, he positioned himself not as a player in the Washington game but as a detached, observant critic of the not-so-reputable scene around him.

Talent like this deserves to be recognized. We opened this study of practical politics watching the rise of the country's most legendary retailer, Lyndon Johnson. We saw the "Johnson treatment" and how it made grown men into little tail-wagging cocker spaniels. Ronald Reagan deserves to be the other bookend in this narrative. As an aide to his prime adversary, House Speaker Tip O'Neill, I spent a great deal of time trying to plumb the "Great Communicator's" depths, to answer that old question LBJ used to put to people, "How'd *he* get there?"

The answer in this case is not that he spent hours meeting people one-to-one as the Great Retailer. No, Ronald Reagan is a man of the media: the Great Wholesaler.

This is not meant as a criticism. My grandfather-in-law, Henry Stueck, was a lifelong salesman. His favorite maxim is, "There's only two professions: statesmanship and salesmanship." With respect, I'd say there is only *one*—and Ronald Reagan has mastered it. Other leaders have taught us the Horatio Alger truism that you can be anything you want to be, go as far as you want to go. The Great Wholesaler has taught us the video-age equivalent: you can *position* yourself anywhere you want to be.

This is hardly meant as a criticism. It is the secret of this immensely successful man's career. Where other politicians cannot wait to be seen as political professionals, the man from the West had a smarter ambition for the 1980s: to stay an *outsider*. The rule he teaches is that anyone, individual or corporation, can establish a position at will.

A new CEO can make himself "just another employee of the firm" or its aloof and commanding eminence. Avis can rent huge numbers of cars by saying "We're No. 2" and thereby appeal to the underdog in all of us. Pepsi-Cola can call itself "the drink of the new generation"; Coke can position itself as an American "classic"; in both these cases, the soft-drink company is battling for a greater market share by positioning itself in an era marked by rapid cultural change.

Ronald Reagan knows the same game. Far from being spontaneous, his status as a political outsider was the result of conscious strategy. He has *positioned* himself to increase his market share, not by trying to be "one of the boys" but by being part of the TV audience he cherishes.

The first person to recognize this Reagan play was, not so surprisingly, the first to face him politically, former Governor Pat Brown of California, the first man Reagan ever beat for public office. "He is the self-appointed leader of '*us*,' " wrote Brown years after his 1966 defeat by Reagan, "and the enemy is always '*them*.' "

Most of Reagan's critics have failed to digest this. They knock him as a "B-movie actor," ignoring not only the quality of his present performance, but his earlier career.

Ronald Reagan did not take up a role when he entered politics; he simply continued to play the role he had played so many years in private life.

Many people overlook the fact that the "Great Communicator" earned his wide national fame not on the movie screen but on the television tube. People got to know him not at their neighborhood theaters but in their own living rooms. By the millions they grew used to him in a far more intimate role than that of actor. Rather than see him playing someone else, they saw him appear to play himself: "Your host, Ronald Reagan."

Reagan's greatest luck is that his adversaries never

caught on to this. When he was introducing his winning personality during the 1950s and the early 1960s, they were out hitting the chicken-dinner circuit. They never earned that Reagan succeeded not simply because he possesses winsome good looks, charm and wit, but because he used his natural gifts in the service of a very particular strategy. He knows exactly where he wants to stand in the public mind.

During his eight years on the old *General Electric Theater*, Reagan enjoyed certain distinct professional advantages. The program's other performers were at the mercy of the weekly dramatic material—it was an anthology series—but the star/host was not. He was no more responsible for the quality of the shows than he was for the quality of GE's products. It was Reagan who ended each show with the famous sign-off, "Here at General Electric, progress is our most important product." That "here" was located at some imaginary point between General Electric and your home. My strongest memory of *GE Theater* twenty-five years later is the image of the host and his wife, Nancy, sitting side by side in the spacious living room of their "totally electric home." They looked a little bit better off, perhaps, than most of the audience, but they did not seem in any important way different from us. In fact, they personified what we wanted to be, or what we wanted to *have*.

Reagan retained the same intermediary position in politics. His press conferences offer a clear illustration.

For years, we watched the Washington press corps grill Nixon, Ford or Carter. We saw our Presidents sweat and grimace like the accused in a murder trial. Nixon, in particular, always looked as if he had just been hauled in from the lockup. From the beginning, Reagan was determined to make things different. He and his advisers never lost sight of the primary message sent in any Presidential news conference: *who the President is.*

First of all, he was likable, relaxed, still the host of his television show. He is not some loner who hides away in a White House back office. And to convey this message, he exploited some off-camera tools of the TV age.

Did you ever wonder how Reagan at his press conferences always seemed to know the names of the reporters? It was as if he spent a lot of time hanging out with the boys. The truth was, he used the White House press corps to persuade the audience at home what a regular guy he is. No matter who the reporter, no matter how obscure the newspaper, the President always seems to know "Joe" or "Bob" or "Ann" on a chummy, first-name basis.

Those who are shaken by Reagan's brain-dead memory in other matters—the Iran-contra hearings come to mind —may be surprised. But where his predecessors spent the precious minutes before press conferences prepping themselves on government policy, foreign and domestic, Ronald Reagan had a seating chart and before going on camera he checked a closed-circuit-television monitor scanning the Joes, Bobs and Anns. He was thus able to get a fix on the location of each reporter with whom he intended to exchange a few pleasantries or thrusts that evening. Having matched nicknames with faces, and faces with seats, he was ready to go on the air.

Reagan's system wasn't foolproof. At a press conference, in early 1984, the President looked down into the audience and called out, "Pat!" The intended target, Patrick McGrath of the Metromedia network, said later that at first he couldn't believe the friendly diminutive was addressed to him. He had no reason to assume that the President knew his name, especially since he was quite clearly looking at the row just behind, but after a moment of uncertainty McGrath stood and asked his question.

Let's face it. There is no way in the world that a reporter, blinded with the prime-time national TV camera, is going to try anything "tricky" at such a moment. With the boys back in the newsroom hooting and stomping, the man in the spotlight is not about to kill the fun. Besides, after a guy gets called on—by nickname, no less!—by the President of the United States, his job becomes a tad more secure than it was a few seconds before.

At one press conference, the President even went so far as to introduce three new members of the White House press corps family. For a moment it was like watching a TV quizmaster welcome a couple of new guests to the show.

But the preparations for press conferences pale before the state-of-the-art technology used when Ronald Reagan gives a televised speech to Congress on TV.

Speaker Tip O'Neill received a letter several years ago from a lady upset about the dangers posed by the President's apparent determination to give forty-five-minute speeches without notes. What would happen, she worried, if the President were to make a mistake on a matter of grave international importance?

But of course there was nothing remotely impromptu about such addresses. Whenever Reagan addressed Congress, the House must recess an hour and a half early to give White House communications aides time to rig up the President's remarkable TelePrompTers. Unlike previous Presidents, Reagan had his two prompter screens arrayed very wide apart. This allowed him to pivot from one to the other, giving the appearance of addressing the entire chamber while keeping the prompters themselves safely out of camera range. The public at home saw only a man giving a polished oration, addressing both sides of the audience. The President, debonair in his contact lenses, gave no indication that he was reading. In fact, the prompters, set intentionally high, helped him appear more *youthful* by keeping his eyes wider open.

Only rarely, in an occasional wide shot, did we see the

two glass plates. But on our home television screens they looked like bulletproof security shields.

The President took his TelePrompTer with him wherever he went, but it would be a mistake to ascribe the Great Communicator's skills to technology alone. He was, first of all, a skilled and professional performer who did not skimp on rehearsal time, spending vital hours at the front of the White House family movie theater mastering his material. By the time he delivered his speeches, his command was so great that TV viewers could not even see the pupils of his eyes pause on the TelePrompTer screen; his rotation was so smooth that it looked to all appearances as if his eyes were locked on his audience, not on the words being projected on the glass.

Above all, he never forgot that he himself, not "supply-side economics" or "strategic defense," was the most important product. Backstage monitors were there to help him appear more "regular" and less regal. The space-age TelePrompting and those contacts of his made him more *personal* in his broadcasts.

When Reagan used such techniques, he was positioning himself with enormous science, establishing himself in the public mind not as an aloof head of government but as the man next door. Every action was designed to make him appear close to the people and distant from the government. Where his predecessors identified themselves with the attainment of government power, Reagan posed as a visiting citizen. Announcing for reelection, he referred to the Presidency rather distantly as "the office I now hold." When he went on vacation, he made no bones about it.

Visualize the competing lifestyles of the two most recent Presidents from California. When Richard Nixon went home, he held court at "the Western White House." In other words, he brought the office with him. Remember the pictures we saw of Nixon in California: a solitary man walking the beaches of San Clemente, head bowed with the burdens of high office, wearing black wing-tipped shoes. When Ronald Reagan went home, he went to the "ranch," wore plaid shirt, jeans and boots, and rode around in a Jeep. We spotted him, through a telescopic lens, on his way to clear brush or repair a fence. Tucked back in those mountains, he made no pretense of being a chief executive on leave: there was an engaging quality of playing hooky from the job. Yet Reagan was the man who had sought great office for more than two decades, the man who presided over the largest bureaucracy in American history.

Pundits have spent years trying to figure out how Ronald Reagan escaped responsibility for the government's problems and mistakes. The simple answer is that he refused to be seen as part of that government. He rejected it the way some organisms reject foreign tissue. Ronald Reagan did not rise to the Presidency, he redefined it. He made it not the job of running the government—those chores were left to dispensable figures such as Ann Burford or Alexander Haig or Margaret Heckler or Don Regan—but simply the job of being Ronald Reagan.

He was, of course, by no means the first American politician to engage in a bit of political positioning: he simply refined the technique. George McGovern won the 1972 Democratic Presidential nomination largely because he positioned himself ideologically, making it clear that he stood to the left of every other candidate on the issue of Vietnam. This position gave him the troops to wage a successful campaign against the party's more prominent leaders, which unfortunately made it easy for Richard Nixon and Spiro T. Agnew to claim the political center a few months later.

In the same way, Senator Gary Hart jumped to an early if brief lead in 1984 by positioning himself as the breezy candidate of "new ideas," the representative of a new generation of Democrat. Wearing a plaid shirt, jeans and boots —shades of Reagan?—he engaged in a little "photo opportunity" in which he threw an ax at a tree stump. The real target was the gray, entrenched "insiders" of the Democratic Party establishment. He used his L. L. Bean image as a direct shot at Walter Mondale, the lawyerly Brooks Brothers candidate. The former VP himself admitted that he came off as rather "official."

Ronald Reagan sought and accomplished a far more subtle positioning. It is important to recall that this enormously popular man came to office facing a grave set of challenges. Starting with Lyndon Johnson, the public had seen four Presidencies destroyed within twelve years by Vietnam, Watergate, Iran. Reagan was determined to define the office, not to let it define him.

Ronald Reagan had witnessed the bitter undoing of a President who had tried to carry too much baggage. Rejecting the role of head of state, Jimmy Carter had made himself entirely a head of government. Having denied himself the grander trappings of office—he ordered that "Hail to the Chief" not be played at his arrivals—he allowed himself to take personal responsibility for everything that went wrong. Faced with double-digit inflation, he created a White House "Office of Inflation." When fifty Americans were taken hostage in Iran, he allowed the quest for their release to swallow his entire Presidency. He carried the burdens of office as he did his own garment bag.

Ronald Reagan made sure the public knew from the start that he was elected to work in Washington, but he was not *of* Washington. He would be the country's head of state, not some national custodian answerable every time the power failed or the toilet overflowed. He had said in his acceptance speech, "Government is not the solution to our problem, it's the problem." He would not allow himself to become part of that problem, never let anyone doubt that Ronald Reagan's home was in California, not Washington, D.C. As late as August 1986, he would be able to attend the Illinois State Fair posing as some cowpoke from the West. "One of the great things about being at this state fair," he told an appreciative crowd, "is that maybe I can tell a joke they wouldn't understand as well in Washington."

In moments like this, Ronald Reagan was not simply setting up a criticism. He was portraying himself as something subtly different from a conventional Chief Executive. He was placing himself not in government but at some unique point—previously uncharted—between government and us. This gave him valuable distance when disaster struck, when programs failed, when his appointees did embarrassing things.

It was no accident that Reagan chose the previously overlooked medium of radio to address the nation each week. Each Saturday he chose a different topic, but the message was generally the same. No matter what was ailing the country, those who tuned in at 12:05 P.M. EST heard the same offstage "they" being called on the carpet. Each Saturday, that Iowa-trained radio voice came to us bristling with complaints about government—the dread purveyor of deficits, crime, red tape and other evils. Listening to him, it was easy to forget that this Paul-Harvey-on-the-Potomac was the head of the federal government. As a disembodied voice—the White House refused to allow the broadcast session to be televised—he became a kind of national neighbor, concerned as we all were about the way things were going. The timing was critical. Since Saturday is not a workday, the President was off duty, removed from the Washington power structure.

The radio addresses presented a perfect opportunity for

Reagan to skip town on whatever ticklish issue was hovering above the Oval Office. It was across this back fence that the President was free to denounce the shabby treatment given his good friend James G. Watt at the hands of the media and the far-out environmentalists. Tuning in, one would never know that this indignant commentator was actually the same man who had briskly snapped up the former Interior Secretary's resignation for having made some insensitive, well-publicized remarks about his appointment of "a black, a woman, two Jews and a cripple" to a federal advisory panel.

As we saw in late 1986, the technique can be badly employed. Faced with undeniable evidence that profits from the Iran arms deal had been funneled to the Nicaraguan contras, Reagan fired Colonel Oliver North from the National Security Council staff. Three days later, he declared the same North a "national hero." He should have waited a few weeks as in the case of Jim Watt, before trying to reposition himself as an aggrieved third party to the affair.

His proven ability to reposition himself a safe distance from official Washington had protected him again and again from the traditional dangers of incumbency. When an American barracks was car-bombed in Beirut, the President stepped aside from the disaster: the Marines could not be blamed, because they were in the process of fortifying the barracks area, but "like a kitchen being refurbished, it's never done as soon as you would like." In a subsequent State of the Union Message, he gave a pointed reminder that *Congress* had authorized the placement of troops in Lebanon, ignoring the fact that he had for several months made support of his peacekeeping mission an acid test of patriotism.

Previous Presidents have held tight to the trappings of office, but Ronald Reagan had fought hard to keep free.

His role as author of the federal budget is one example. The President who never submitted a balanced budget went twice to Capitol Hill during 1982 to lead balance-the-budget *rallies*. Standing at the head of the angry crowd, he presented himself simply as an average citizen, concerned, just like everybody else, at the rising flood of red ink. Two years later, the man who had presided over a doubling of the national debt stood comfortably at his alma mater, Eureka College, and demanded, "Politicians at the national level must no longer be permitted to mortgage your future."

Reagan's mastery of positioning has to be envied by his predecessors, one in particular.

Think back to the 1968 Republican national convention. The party's nominee for President was giving the speech of his life. Having finished with the main body of his address, he shifted pace, becoming uncharacteristically intimate with the national audience. Switching to the third person, he began to narrate the story of a boy growing up with limited prospects in a small town in southern California. His voice began to quake. "He hears the train go by at night, and he dreams of faraway places he would like to go. It seems like an impossible dream . . ."

Now the climax. That boy with his head on the pillow at night listening to the Western Pacific rush by, that dreamer of the "impossible dream," was now standing before the thousands of delegates. "Tonight he stands before you nominated for President of the United States of America. You can see now why I believe so deeply in the American dream." Even Nixon-haters were impressed.

It seemed totally spontaneous, but behind the scenes there was craft. In a hotel room later that night Nixon allowed himself some credit for the speech's great close. "I'd like to see Rocky or Romney or Lindsay do a moving thing like that 'impossible dream' part, where I changed my voice, he said to aide William Safire. Reagan's an actor, but I'd like to see *him* do it."

Twelve years later he did, at the 1980 Republican national convention. The words with which Reagan accepted the nomination may not claim many lines in the history books, but the music of the speech was soaring.

The climactic moment came as Reagan appeared to end his prepared remarks. He paused on the platform, looked out to the convention floor and to the millions at home, and announced that, in the best Hollywood tradition, he was throwing away the script.

"I have just thought of something that is not part of my speech," Reagan said in his best husky-intimate voice, "and I am worried whether I should do it."

He paused again, and followed through with a beautifully composed tribute to America as the refuge of those "who yearn to breathe freely." Then the clincher: "I'll confess that I'm a little afraid to suggest what I am going to suggest. I'm more afraid not to."

He then asked for a moment of silent prayer for the great "crusade" he was now beginning.

Reagan's finale was the hit of the convention. It had drama, suspense, even a Hitchcockian twist at the end, all of which dynamized the politics of the occasion. It allowed Reagan to do what he likes to do most: portray himself as an amateur among professionals, a citizen among politicians. Only later would it get out that the finale had been written well ahead of time. The closing remarks, which had been purposefully deleted from the texts given to the press, were on his three-by-five cards all the time.

Perspective

At a black-tie "roast" of New Jersey Senator Bill Bradley of New Jersey held in 1987, his colleague Albert Gore of Tennessee told the following tale:

Senator Bradley came to the Senate with his reputation as Princeton All-American and National Basketball Association star preceding him. Invited to make a speech at a large banquet, the confident legislator sat at the head table waiting to make his address.

When the waiter came around and put a pat of butter on his plate, Bradley stopped him. "Excuse me. Can I have two pats of butter?"

"Sorry," the waiter said, "one pat to a person."

"I think you don't know who I am, Bradley said. "I'm BILL BRADLEY, the Rhodes Scholar, professional basketball player, world champion, United States Senator."

The waiter said, "Well, maybe you don't know who I am."

"Well, as a matter of fact I don't," Bradley said. "Who are you?"

"I'm the guy," the waiter said, "who's in charge of the *butter*."

In the world of power, there's always someone you have to deal with.

Index

About the Author

Christopher Matthews began his political career as an aide to Senator Frank Moss of Utah. He went on to join the staff of the Senate Budget Committee, became a speechwriter for President Jimmy Carter and then, for six years, was the chief spokesman for former House Speaker Thomas P. (Tip) O'Neill. He recently served as CEO of The Government Research Corporation, an organization that advises corporations on how to get things done in Washington. Currently, Christopher Matthews is the Washington Bureau Chief for the *San Francisco Examiner* and a syndicated columnist for *King Features,* and his political commentary is a regular feature of the *Larry King Show.*